NEWS FOR THE 99%

2

Solidarity forever
Tim Wheeler
Oct, 2020

NEWS FOR THE 99%

VOLUME 2

TIM WHEELER

Published by International Publishers.

First Edition 2020

ISBN-10 0-7178-0764-9   ISBN-13 978-0-7178-0764-2
Typeset by Amnet Systems, Chennai, India

Footprints on Mora Beach

I see you came this way, your bare feet
pressed into the wet sand, toes, ball of each foot,
heels, sharp and clear, walking north on Mora Beach,
north of the Quileute, north of LaPush.
You turned and looked back, James Island tall at the river
mouth, lit by the morning sun. We will remember you now,
before the tide washes near and the edges crumble
where your footsteps fell.
Soon the footprints will be gone, fading like family albums,
like your memory, shrouded in the mist of Alzheimers.
Only this shall remain: The shore, long and wide, surf
pounding, waves draining back, a sucking sound, down the
pebbled beach at ebb tide.
The sea stacks loom like dark cathedrals in the Pacific. And
on that rough reach of sand and littered stones, seaweed,
kelp, driftwood, seagulls cry, we know you walked here once.
You held earthly treasures
in your heart, of open space not walls of hate and fear and
greed. A thousand African American children you taught to
read in Baltimore. You taught these little ones in the dawn
of life to nourish all creatures, to love dearly all living souls,
all sisters and brothers, fathers and mothers and their young
ones. Joyce, my beloved, we walk in your footsteps
up this shore, hope singing in our hearts, like fresh winds
ripple a becalmed sea.
We are alive.
We live to make your dreams come real.

Tim Wheeler
Sequim, July 28, 2019

In Memoriam

TW.

Joyce Provost Wheeler
1941-2019

Table of Contents

Foreword

Tim Wheeler's news stories written over half a century restore faith in the magnificent accomplishments of the broad united democratic, progressive forces in the United States. The Communist Party USA, now celebrating its 100th birthday, has been and will always be a leading part of that great mass struggle.

Tim's writings remind the reader that the class struggle is and will remain a basic reality of life and survival for workers and oppressed people everywhere. I know this from personal experience because I have been an eyewitness, a close friend and comrade of Tim and his beloved Joyce since I first met them when Tim was a student at Amherst College in 1964. I was on an organizing bus trip through New England recruiting young people to attend the founding convention of the W.E.B. DuBois Clubs in San Francisco later that summer. Tim and Joyce organized a meeting of about twenty students from Amherst College, UMASS, Smith and Mount Holyoke.

We met again in 1967 when I was elected President of the DuBois Clubs and moved with my family to New York. By then, Tim was a reporter for the Worker. We lived around the corner from them in the Crown Heights neighborhood of Brooklyn. My son, Keith, became a bosom buddy of Tim and Joyce's sons, Morgan and Nick. We have worked together in the class struggle ever since.

Massive resistance is sweeping across the globe today. From teachers to Auto workers, US workers of all races and nationalities are more ready and willing to strike for a better life today.

The call for impeachment of President Donald Trump is gaining majority support in this country.

I think pressure is building because US Capitalism is in a deeper crisis, the democratic gains won by the working people over the past century are menaced by ruthless corporate profit greed personified by Donald Trump.

As Tim's writing shows, the political seeds for today's resistance were planted over many decades of struggle. The great point in Tim's working-class journalism is basic, the people have been and will continue to fight because, that is the only way they can win. They have no choice.

Millions are marching for justice and freedom around the world. The house of Trump is collapsing in the face of its criminal impeachable misdeeds. Millions are learning and relearning that the class struggle is real and unstoppable.

Reading Tim Wheeler's articles from the *Worker*, The *Daily World* and the *Peoples World*, should be mandatory for anyone concerned about Peace, justice and the advancement of humanity.

Of course, setbacks happen but setbacks are not permanent. Neither are victories for that matter.

What was built under Eastern European Socialism was built on the ashes of Czarism and Fascism. Through the articles of Tim Wheeler, we are reminded of that reality that change is constant. Socialism in that part of the world unfortunately was dismantled and set-back. But, it can, and I believe will be rebuilt and made stronger and better.

In our country today it is gaining more mass support than perhaps ever before and our country is not the only country where this is happening. Socialism is gaining in popularity in our country today, especially among our youth.

Reading Tim Wheeler's excellent articles about the great civil rights battles in the deep South one realizes the deep relationship between the class and national struggle. The struggle continues and the unity of Labor and civil rights is transformative for the South, united with all the great democratic movements of our time, it will change the nation as a whole.

2020 can be a big turning point if democratic forces unite and keep on pushing.

The lessons of history are real and alive in Wheeler's writings. Thank you Tim for making a tremendous contribution to the fight for freedom and socialism.

You and Joyce have given a lifetime to the working class and our Party. You should know, Tim, that you are not alone in mourning the death of Joyce, a staunch union teacher, loving wife and mother, and a gracious hostess over many years for the hundreds of visitors to your home in Baltimore, people on their way to mass demonstrations in Washington, D.C. The enormous contributions that the Wheeler family, especially Tim and Joyce, is deeply appreciated by many across this nation and globe.

When I read your memoirs I think of the greatness of our Party and the 100 years of courageous efforts and great sacrifices our comrades have made.

Through his reportage and activism, Tim Wheeler helps us see the reality of how political struggle and grassroots activism can bend the great Arc of Humanity towards justice.

"News for the 99%," both vol. 1 and 2 are a must read.

Jarvis Tyner
November, 2019

Preface

Toward Singing Tomorrows

As I write, we are entering the third week of President Trump's shut-down of the Federal Government, idling 800,000 Federal workers who are either furloughed without pay or working without compensation like thousands of TSA airport screeners.

Unable to bully the Democratic leadership to surrender and give him his $5.6 billion wall along the Mexican border, Trump is now muttering that he could declare a "National Emergency." This is an attempt to get his way by Presidential diktat, a dangerous abuse of power. There is no national emergency on the Southern border. The emergency is inside the White House. His power grab, with more than a "whiff of fascism," is a "high crime" an impeachable offense.

The Southern border crisis is Trump's flailing attempt to nullify his crushing defeat in the Nov. 6 midterm elections. A powerful grassroots movement, spearheaded by women, had been building for two years since Trump's election by the Electoral College. It was a movement that rejected Trump's misogyny, racism, hatred of immigrants, his obsession with a wall aimed at blocking refugees fleeing gang violence. His foreign policy is unilateralism to promote the U.S. as a ruthless global cop.

Trump is a billionaire, or at least close to it. His economic policies, his tax policies have picked the pockets of working people and filled to overflowing the pockets of his billionaire cronies. Never in our history have we confronted such a menacing threat to basic democratic rights. Every gain we have won in the past century are at risk of being taken away.

Those were the stakes in this midterm election. Consider the results: Democrats outpolled the Republicans by nearly nine million votes. That compares to 2016 when Democrat Hillary Clinton, outpolled Trump by nearly three million votes in the race for the presidency. The Republicans lost majority control of the House last November when the broad democratic coalition flipped 40 seats from "red" to "blue." The Democrats also flipped seven governorships including the ouster of the Wisconsin's Republican Governor Scott Walker. The grassroots voter movement flipped nearly 400 state legislative seats and won a 27 to 51 majority of Attorney General races.

The milestones were many: More than 100 women sworn in as members of the U.S. House of Representatives, the most in history; the first Muslim woman. The first two Native American Indian women. The first open Lesbian woman. Alexandria Ocasio-Cortez, a self-described socialist was elected.

Many of the candidates were first-time contenders, had never been involved in politics before. The candidates ran issue-oriented campaigns demanding health health care for all, $15 an hour living wage jobs, immigration reform with a path to citizenship for 11 million undocumented immigrants: an end "gun violence" and National Rifle Association "dark money." They denounced oil, gas, and coal company schemes to preserve U.S. dependence on fossil fuels and demanded "green energy" to counter global climate change. They defended Roe v. Wade and reproductive rights of women and marriage equality for LGBQT couples.

The movement made inroads into regions long controlled by the Republicans even in races they did not win. Stacey Abrams, Democrat, the first African American woman to run for governor in Georgia refused to concede to her Republican opponent, Brian Kemp. The vote margin was razor thin. At one point after the polls closed, it was Kemp, 1,978,408 to Abrams, 1,923,685, a margin of only 54,723 for Kemp, surprisingly close to the 53,000 mostly African American voters Kemp removed from voter rolls. He was serving as Secretary of State in charge of conducting the election, including his own. Similarly, Andrew Gillum, the first Black gubernatorial candidate in Florida came within a whisker of defeating his Republican opponent, Ron DeSantis, a Trump lackey. Rep. Beto O'Roarke nearly unseated the scowling incumbent Senator, Ted Cruz, in Texas. Not forgotten is the victory in a special U.S. senate race in Alabama of Democrat Doug Jones over the child molester Republican, Judge Roy Moore. Alabama is the most Republican state in the nation.

The results underlined that the Democratic Party has shifted to the left. The mass movements that turned out tens of millions to vote against the Republicans is politically independent. Yet these movements are also in the orbit of the Democratic Party. In the Rev.Jesse Jackson's phrase, the Democrats are a "big tent" party. The watchwords are "unity" and "independence."

The struggle is far from over. Trump refuses to yield, lurching instead to the right, embracing more and more open authoritarian measures to assert his tyrannical powers.

Yet I am rejoicing at the midterm election results. I join with the grassroots movements that urges the Democratic leadership to stand its ground, not yield an inch to Trump. Not a penny for his border wall. We need billions to rebuild roads and bridges, not build walls.

I have a personal reason for rejoicing, My entire half century as a reporter-editor for the Worker, Daily World, People's Weekly World and online People's World is summed up in this midterm election. The theme running through all my writing was the struggle by the labor movement, the civil rights movement, the peace movement, the environmetal movement to defend democracy, to break the grip of the corporate rightwing on our lives. I have selected about 100 of my best stories reflecting this glorious struggle of our people in defense of democracy. These were not struggles for socialism, the form of democratic governance that I uphold. Yet in my opinion, each of these struggles brings socialism closer. The French poet, Louis Aragon called it "toward singing tomorrows." I am singing!

NEWS FOR THE 99%

Chapter 1

I Win Friends in the D.C. Press Corps

President Obama and Helen Thomas, Dean of the White House Press Corps, share cup cakes in the press briefing room. Their birthdays are on the same day. Thomas turned 89 and Obama 48. Photo by Pete Souza, White House photographer

Helen Thomas Comes to My Rescue

People's World, Sept. 26, 2014
THE TELEPHONE RANG in my office in the National Press Building. On the line was Gus Hall, National Chairman of the Communist Party USA. This must have been sometime in 1977 or 1978.

Luis Corvalan, the exiled leader of the Communist Party of Chile, had applied for a visa to visit the U.S. and had been rejected. "Is there anything you can do to help out?" Hall asked.

I was at a loss for words. "Well Gus, I can go to the White House press briefing today and ask President Carter's press secretary. That's about the only thing I can think of."

So I did. My White House Press Pass entitled me to attend the daily briefings and Presidential news conferences. Yet the White House was hardly my favorite destination.

It was so stage-managed. Each of the seats in the Press Briefing room had a brass plate attached to it with the name of the correspondent and the newspaper, news agency or network he or she represented. At that time, the White House press corps mostly sat around waiting for the Press Office to distribute a press release.

Yet I was conscious of the ordeal Luis Corvalan had endured. His Party—and Corvalan personally—were part of the broad coalition that elected Salvador Allende as the first socialist president of Chile in 1970.

General Augusto Pinochet and his minions overthrew Allende's democratic election in 1973 with the full connivance of President Richard Nixon, National Security Adviser Henry Kissinger, and the Central Intelligence Agency (CIA).

Corvalan went into hiding. The fascists arrested and tortured Corvalan's son, Alfredo, who died of the wounds.

The fascists tracked Corvalan down. He was tried and convicted of "high treason" but a worldwide outcry forced Pinochet to back off from executing him. In 1976, the Pinochet regime released Corvalan in exchange for the Soviet release of dissident, Vladimir Bukovsky.

Corvalan went into exile in Moscow and it was there that he applied for a visa to tour the U.S.

As I walked along Pennsylvania Avenue to the West Wing of the White House, I turned over in my mind Nixon's instigation of fascist coups around the world, not to speak of the Watergate coup right here in Washington. President Jimmy Carter's pose as a champion of democracy, lecturing the Soviet Union and other socialist countries on their alleged abuse of "human rights," was hypocrisy at its crudest.

When I entered the Press Briefing Room, I stood at the back, behind all the assigned seats.

Press Secretary Jody Powell was in his usual smart aleck mode, kidding the reporters, one wise crack after another.

The press corps asked all their questions, often the same question asked in a dozen different ways. The session was coming to an end.

I raised my hand. Powell called on me. "Luis Corvalan, leader of the Communist Party of Chile has applied for a visa to visit the United States and has been rejected by the State Department. In light of the President's call for upholding human rights, can you explain why the visa was denied?"

Powell listened to my question with a bored expression and then snapped, "When Brezhnev stops persecuting Doctor Andrei Sakharov and hounding Alexander Solzhenitsyn we'll have an answer for you."

The press corps broke into embarrassed giggles at Powell's witticism.

"You haven't answered my question," I replied.

"Well, I've given you as good as you're going to get," Powell replied. There were more titters from the reporters.

Then, at the front of the room, a woman spoke up in a loud, commanding voice. "He's right, you haven't answered the question."

It was Helen Thomas, dean of the Press Corps, White House correspondent for United Press International who had covered every president since Dwight Eisenhower.

Powell turned ashen white and the smirk disappeared from his face. The briefing room fell silent.

In a polite voice, Powell told me, "I don't know the answer. But I will take your question."

In press corps jargon, it meant that Powell was promising to get an answer, and call me back. (He never did,
despite my repeated calls to the White House.)

I pushed my way to the front of the Press Briefing
room, leaned over and whispered to Helen Thomas.
"Thank you."

I encountered Helen Thomas many times in the years
that followed. Often she was dining with a coterie of
cub reporters at a nearby table in a modest restaurant
in Georgetown or some other neighborhood. I would
congratulate her for her sharp questioning during Presidential press conferences. By tradition, she asked the
first question. She was of Lebanese background and
sometimes asked pointed questions on why the U.S.
gave billions of dollars in military aid to Israel, no questions asked.

On that day, Helen Thomas proved herself a defender
of freedom of the press, and a defender, as well of democracy in Chile.

My 15 Minutes of Fame

September 29, 2014
IN 1984-1985, THE NATIONAL PRESS CLUB decided to
drastically revamp the old National Press Building (NPB)
where the *People's Daily World* had its modest one-room
office. One reason for the existence of the NPB was to
provide affordable office space for struggling newspapers like ours. But the media moguls had decided on a
policy of ruthless consolidation, the giant fish gobbling
up the small fry. Our office was to be demolished. The
space we had once rented for about $500 monthly would
rent for well over $1,000 monthly.

We decided to close the office. I would move to the
House Press Gallery on Capitol Hill. I was sorry to lose
the office, only a five-minute walk from the White House.
But there were many pluses. The space in the House
Press Gallery was free. It eliminated the last leg of my
commuting. When I rolled into town every morning on

SHINGTON POST   THURSDAY, MARCH 8, 1990 A25

ERAL PAGE

Washington Journal

Rowing Against Anti-Communist Tide

By Dale Russakoff
Washington Post Staff Writer

Tim Wheeler, along with half the town, had the flu last week. But it wasn't just the local epidemic that laid him low. His weakened state, he said only half in jest, was partly due to last week's elections in Nicaragua and Lithuania—neither of which went his way.

Wheeler is the Washington correspondent for the People's Daily World, the newspaper of the Communist Party USA. It is his goal to keep hope alive, as Jesse L. Jackson would say, for the party faithful. But with an epidemic of anti-communism sweeping from Vilnius to Bucharest to Managua and with his newspaper in tough financial straits, it isn't easy.

"People up here kid me and say, 'With communism falling everywhere, are you going to go next?'" Wheeler said from his post in the Capitol's House Press Gallery. "They say I should go into business or something."

Far from a joyless ideologue, Wheeler, 50, seems to relish the ribbing. He has been called "the man without a country—except maybe Albania." Also: "The last guy rooting for Castro."

He says the teasing makes him feel as if he belongs. And indeed he does. He has worked in the Capitol press corps since 1968, a culture with a fondness for anyone with endurance. There are trade press reporters who have spent years following sagas of slurry pipelines. There are hometown reporters who cover only news of interest to their far-away readers. There are big-time Washington reporters who feast on Washington power struggles, ignoring anything that affects real people.

And there is Wheeler. Hardly distinguishable in appearance from the rest of the press

proaches a story from the same angle as the pack. When President Bush delivered his State of the Union address and most reporters focused on his call for troop reductions, Wheeler

BY PETER HOLT—THE WASHINGTON POST

pounced on his bid for a cut in the capital gains tax. "Bush Address Masks Handouts to the Rich," blared the headline on his story.

From his sickbed in Baltimore, in the aftermath of the Sandinista defeat, Wheeler raspily interviewed Sandinista sympathizers and filed a report attributing the outcome largely to resignation in the face of suffering caused by the U.S.-backed war there. "The Nicaraguan people were forced to choose survival," an official of Nicaragua Network was quoted as saying.

He also used the story to promote a March 24 mass demonstration, which aims to mobilize large numbers of activists on the 10th anniversary of the murder of Roman Catholic Archbishop Oscar Romero in El Salvador.

"Part of what we're doing now is asserting that we're still alive and well—that these setbacks are not going to deter us from carrying on the struggle," Wheeler said.

But the struggle is itself struggling now. Strapped for money, his newspaper has cut back pub-

Wheeler and his wife attend two and three times a week in Baltimore, where they live. "It's one reason I have laryngitis," he said.

"Good people who have devoted their lives to the movement now find themselves disagreeing over very fundamental questions," he said. "They ask, 'Is Gorbachev right?' 'Democracy, what is it?' 'If there is private property in the Soviet Union, and one person hires another, is he an exploiter?'

"I gnash my teeth," he said. "I say yes, they should have consumer goods [in Eastern Europe], they should have VCRs. They should have the right to choose their leaders. But if they become capitalist, there will be a lot of loss—full employment, free education, free medical care, subsidized foods."

Wheeler is a lifer in the movement, born into it on the Olympic Peninsula in Washington state where his father, a dairy farmer, and grandfather, a bricklayer and follower of Eugene Debs, were socialists. He was so accepted there that he was elected president of his student council and went to Amherst College on scholarship. Wheeler's three children grew up going to anti-war demonstrations with him and his wife.

Besides spending numerous evenings at forums with fellow activists, he can often be found trudging door to door in Baltimore, hawking subscriptions to his paper, which prints 15,000 copies on weekdays, 72,000 on weekends. About 1,000 are sent to the Soviet Union, mostly to tourist hotels.

Unlike others Washington correspondents, Wheeler doesn't worry about being read by members of Congress. He gets his "psychic income," as he calls it (he doesn't get much of the other kind) from his cause.

When he sells newspapers, he said, "I point to an article I've written and I say 'You haven't the commuter train from Baltimore, I simply strolled over to the Capitol and there was my "office" crowded with other reporters like myself searching for a hot story.

Soon after that move, I got a surprising telephone call in the Gallery. It was Portia Siegelbaum who had worked with us on the staff of the *Daily World*. She had married a Cuban man and was now living in Havana. She was calling me from there. She worked for Radio Havana Cuba (RHC). Would I agree to serve as an RHC stringer, sharing my stories with RHC listeners?

I was thunderstruck. "Portia," I replied, "I don't speak Spanish."

"That's O.K.," she said. "We will call you once or twice each week. All you need to do is read your story aloud to us over the phone. We will record it and broadcast it on our English Language Service to our North American audience."

I told her I would check with our editors in New York.

They agreed to Portia's suggestion. It led to a mutually agreeable arrangement that lasted for several years.

It was a cause for some amusement in the House Press Gallery because RHC would call the Press Gallery switchboard. The telephone receptionist would then announce over the public address system in the Press Gallery: "Tim Wheeler . . . Havana calling."

I would take my copy to one of the old-style phone booths that lined the wall. I would close the folding door and dictate my story. I should say I tended to bellow my story into the phone thinking that a loud voice was necessary for the message to reach Havana. The result is that everyone in the Press Gallery heard every word.

Those were wonderful days. Soon, I was on a first-name basis with many other reporters. My friendship with progressive minded reporters deepened. It included members of the foreign press corps, especially those from the Soviet media, the German Democratic Republic (East Germany), Czechoslovakia, and Japan. There was a steady stream of visiting reporters from France,

Germany, Norway. I even hosted a young writer from Grenada during the brief rule of a progressive regime in that island nation. He was welcomed into the House Press Gallery and sat beside me looking over my shoulder or working on his own project while he was in Washington.

On a regular basis, a team of film-makers from Europe visited. They were a bold, fearless crew who had traveled into fascist Chile to film the crimes of dictator, Augusto Pinochet, into El Salvador to film Roberto D'Aubisson and his Arena death squad who had murdered Archbishop Oscar Romero, into South Africa to expose the crimes of the Apartheid regime.

Once they stopped in and told me they were headed to Las Vegas to cover a convention of *Soldiers of Fortune* magazine. Their goal was to interview the crazed right-wingers, many of them KKK Klansmen, who attended the SOF gatherings. They stopped back after the convention, elated by their success. They described the gruesome scene: Crazed mercenaries and militiamen waving firearms and guzzling beer from human skulls. The guest-of-honor at the gathering was U.S. Army General Jack Singlaub, a certified fascist. They had secured a lengthy, highly revealing interview with the General who once commanded U.S. forces in South Korea until President Carter fired him for seditious activities.

The films they made were shown throughout Europe. Many were shared with the Soviet Union and other socialist nations. The films played a vital role in exposing the fraudulence in the U.S. pose as a force for freedom and democracy. In fact, their films proved that outright terrorism was at the heart of U.S. foreign and military policy. I helped them get stories when they came to the United States. They became lifelong friends.

Once they came with a difficult and vital assignment. They were working on a film commemorating the 40th anniversary of the Nuremburg Trials of Nazi war criminals. Their film would focus on the role of giant German banks and corporations in bankrolling Adolph Hitler's seizure of power, the role of these same corporations in reaping billions of Reichsmarks from slave labor and war-profiteering during World War II.

Did I have any ideas of people they could interview?

"Yes," I replied. "You should interview Mary Kaufman. She and her husband live in New York City. Mary, an attorney, was a Prosecutor during the Nuremburg Trials. She prepared the indictment of I.G. Farben, the German chemical trust that manufactured Zyclon-B, the deadly gas used to exterminate the Jews during the Holocaust."

As I spoke I could see their eyes grow wide! Within minutes. I reached Mary on the phone, informing her about these filmmakers. They traveled to New York and interviewed Mary at length, producing a film that proved conclusively that I.G. Farben and other German corporations and banks were full, eager, accomplices of Adolph Hitler and the Third Reich. Even though the Potsdam Agreement committed all the allies in the defeat of Hitler to break up these banks and corporations, to "de-Nazify" Germany, the U.S. led the way in returning all these banks and corporations to power behind a curtain of Cold War, anti-Soviet slander.

Henri Alleg, a legendary fighter for Algerian independence, who endured torture at the hands of French fascist paratroopers, editor of *La Republica*, came to ask for my help when he was in Washington gathering material for his book "S.O.S. America." I hesitated. Maybe my close connection with the Communist Party, USA would be more a hindrance than a help especially since the paper he wrote for then, *l'Humanite*, was a respected, mass circulation newspaper in France. Henri agreed to try his best. A week later he called, desperation in his voice. He had hit a brick wall. He could not get any lawmakers to agree to an interview.

"Come to the press gallery tomorrow morning," I told him.

He showed up at about 10 a.m. I used my Press Gallery ID card to get Henri and me into the House Cloak Room just downstairs from the press gallery. I wrote brief notes on the back of my business card: "French writer is seeking interview with you. Can you help?" I gave the business card to the young pages who had access to the House Floor. The pages would hand the card to a Representative. They came out in a steady stream and gave Henri ten or fifteen-minute interviews.

At the end of two hours, he had six or seven interviews. He was elated. We walked out of the Cloak Room and were waiting for the elevator to take us back upstairs. Who should walk up but House Speaker, Jim Wright, Democrat of Texas. Wright knew me well. I was a regular at his morning briefings in his Capitol office. I introduced him to Henri. We stepped away from the elevator and engaged in a cordial discussion for about five minutes.

Wright was a courtly gentleman and he was very friendly to me. He defied President Reagan by meeting with Nicaraguan President Daniel Ortega, seeking to end the deadly contra-war that Reagan had instigated and armed through his secret, illegal Iran-contra conspiracy. The rightwing extremists in the next election concocted a phony real estate scandal that forced Wright to retire.

. . .

My routine was to sit beside other reporters at the long, narrow counter with a telephone in front of me, and my Tandy-200 laptop. I would gather material for my articles, compose them, and transmit them over the phone line to our office in New York.

One morning I was sitting beside Tom Kenworthy, the *Washington Post* Capitol Hill correspondent. His phone rang. It was Dale Russakoff, a *Washington Post* columnist who penned a popular column called *Washington Journal.* Her modus operandi was to call *Post* correspondents on Capitol Hill and all the various agencies in all three branches of government to ask them for tips on a good story for her column.

So she asked Tom: "Do you have any tips for me?"

And I heard Tom reply, "Gee, Dale. I don't know. I can't think of anybody you can interview."

Then he happened to turn in my direction. His eyes lit up. "Why don't you interview Tim Wheeler? He's the only Communist reporter here on Capitol Hill. It would make a great story."

A second later, Tom thrust the phone over to me. "Dale Russakoff wants to talk to you."

She asked for an interview. I agreed on the spot.

We met in the gallery and went down to the little cramped coffee shop in the basement of the Capitol so she could ask me questions undisturbed.

We hit it off immediately. She had grown up in Birmingham Alabama and was strongly sympathetic to the Civil Rights movement. She was witty, smart, and irreverent.

She was greatly amused by my story that I was regularly summoned to the phone in the Gallery with the message "Tim Wheeler . . . Havana calling."

Her story appeared in the March 8, 1990 edition of the Washington Post under a headline, *Rowing Against Anti-Communist Tide*.

My fellow reporters in the Press Gallery slapped me on the back, praising the story. I received calls asking for interviews. Just hours after the story appeared, I was summoned to the Gallery phone. "Tim Wheeler . . . Sam Donaldson calling."

Donaldson was White House correspondent of *ABC News*. I lifted the receiver. "Is that you, Wheeler? I'd like an interview?

"Well . . . When?

"The sooner the better."

"Where?"

"You name it. I'll be there."

I told Donaldson I was headed downtown to interview people picketing a department store demanding higher wages. I was leaving immediately.

"I'll meet you there," Donaldson said.

So I rode the subway downtown and walked to the picketline. As I was interviewing workers on the picketline, a black Cadillac stretch limousine rolled up. Out jumped Donaldson, holding a microphone. His camera crew was close behind.

The workers were chanting as they marched in a circle. Donaldson pulled me aside. "The Soviet Union is collapsing. Isn't this the end of Communism?"

"No, I don't believe so. It is the end of the Cold War. The contradictions of capitalism are sharper than ever. The Cold War blinded people to the class struggle here in the U.S. Now they will see clearly who their real enemy is."

Donaldson grew more and more agitated as I spoke. "You'll never give up!" he exclaimed.

"That's right! We'll never give up."

Sam pumped my hand, leaped back into the limousine and roared off.

The crowd on the picketline had been listening in amazement to this mini-drama and were shaking my hand and congratulating me on my excellent interview. I promised them I would write up the story of their struggle.

When I got back to Capitol Hill, reporters were waiting to hear how it had turned out. I told them I thought it went fine. I was waiting for Donaldson's story to air and so were my fellow reporters in the House Press Gallery.

When the story didn't appear at the promised hour, I telephoned Donaldson. I detected a crestfallen note in his voice as he told me they had decided to scrap the interview in exchange for a full interview with Gus Hall at his home in Yonkers New York.

And sure enough, a week or so later, *ABC News* aired a full story about Gus Hall emphasizing how old he is. The interview with me ended up on the "cutting room floor."

Months after this incident, I received a letter in the mail. The envelope was pretty badly mangled from traveling a long, winding, unpaved road. It was from Cuba, a "thank you" letter from the director of *Radio Havana Cuba*. He praised my work and told me my stories were not only broadcast on their English Language service. They were also translated into Spanish, Portuguese, French, German, Arabic, and Quechua. Quechua? The language of the indigenous peoples of the high Andes! I framed it and hung it on my wall. It is my Pulitzer prize.

I Share a Cab with Senator Barry Goldwater

People's World, Sept. 30, 2014
WASHINGTON--I dashed out of the National Press Building on my way to Capitol Hill to cover a House hearing. I heard a voice behind me. "Hey, Tim. Going to the Hill? Let's share a cab."

It was Mike Kraft, Capitol Hill correspondent for the *Reuters News Agency.* Just then, someone charged past us and grabbed the front door handle of our cab. It was Senator Barry Goldwater of Arizona. He jumped into the front seat and slammed the door.

Not intimidated, Mike said, "Excuse me, Senator, do you mind if we ride with you?"

Goldwater snarled, "I don't give a s......"

So we piled in. All the way to the Hill, Goldwater poured

out a stream of obscenities unprintable in a family newspaper. "Those stupid sons-of-a-bitches," he snarled, his face purple with rage. "The Soviets are full-speed ahead on their SST! It's a race and we're going to come in dead last."

The "stupid sons-of-bitches" were his esteemed colleagues in the Senate, famous for their civility and courtesy. Yet Goldwater could not contain his fury, even against his

Republican brethren, eighteen of whom voted no a day earlier in the fifty-one to forty-six vote to kill the Boeing Supersonic Transport March 25, 1971. Sen. Henry M. Jackson, "the gentleman from Boeing," represented the Democrats in seeking to win passage of legislation to fund the SST. After the vote Jackson glumly announced, "The program is dead."

When we reached the Senate office building, Goldwater pulled out a hundred dollar bill. The cabdriver threw up his arms. "Senator, I can't make change for that." Goldwater crossed his arms and sat glowering in silence.

Mike glanced at me with a faint smile. He shrugged and reached for his wallet, "I'll cover it." Goldwater got out and slammed the door without even thanking Mike. The cabdriver then drove us over to the House side of the Capitol. "That's how he got to be a millionaire," Mike said, "Making other people pay his way."

As we pulled up to the House office building, I reached for my wallet. "No no, put it away," Mike said. "I paid Mr. Capitalism's way. I might as well pay Mr. Communist's way too."

I waited until Goldwater died to write up that encounter with the Republican Party's 1964 presidential standard bearer. "Extremism in the defense of liberty is no vice," he famously snarled in his acceptance speech.

He lost to Democrat Lyndon Johnson in a landslide. Yet Goldwater, in many ways, gave birth to the modern Republican Party dominated by tea party extremism and all manner of bigotry and hate. Goldwater was filled with a venomous hatred toward organized labor, the movements for African American, Latino, and women's equality. And, as it turned out, he was filled also with a venomous hatred of moderates in his own party. Goldwater personified the attitude of tea party Republicans: "My way or the highway."

Those moderate Democrats and Republicans proved they were on the right side in voting down funding for the Supersonic Transport. They spared us from wasting tens of billions of tax dollars on an airborne Edsel. The Soviets junked their TU-144 SST. And the French-British consortium mothballed their fleet of SSTs after squandering billions in trying to keep the Concorde alive.

I will always remember what I learned from that cab ride to Capitol Hill: Millionaires get rich by arranging for other people to pay their way.

Chapter *2*

Into the South

Coretta Scott King (center) leads march of striking Charleston hospital workers in 1969. On King's left is Mary Moultrie, President of the Charleston Local 1199. Avery Research Center

Mother Emanuel AME: Mourning 9 Who Died

June 19, 2015

IN THE SPRING of 1969, *Daily World* editors asked me to travel down to Charleston, South Carolina to cover a strike by hospital workers, Local 1199. I took the night train. The strikers, virtually all African American women, staged a massive rally at "Mother Emanuel" AME Church.

I was conscious that this was a place laden with history. It was in this church that the Reverend Denmark

Vesey planned a slave revolt in 1822. He and his five compatriots were hanged. This was the state that sent Senator John C. Calhoun to Washington, the chief ideologue of chattel slavery, who dreamed of a slave empire that encompassed the entire western hemisphere as far south as Tierra del Fuego. From the artillery emplacements along the battery, the Confederates fired on Fort Sumter in Charleston Bay, April 12, 1861, igniting the Civil War.

Mary Moultrie, leader of the Charleston strike was soft-spoken yet the crowd greeted her speech with a standing ovation. These women were seeking a living wage, dignity on the job. "Mother Emanuel" was their sanctuary.

The governor had declared a "State of Emergency," ordering the South Carolina National Guard into Charleston, turning the lovely city into an armed camp. Ruling circles in South Carolina were determined to smash 1199 in their drive to preserve the South as a "Union-Free Environment."

Forty-six years later, "Mother Emanuel" AME is back in the news. Nine African American women and men, worshipping peacefully in the church were murdered in an act of racist terrorism by a white supremacist who invaded the sanctuary and opened fire.

Who killed them? The answer from the ruling powers will be that the killer acted alone, a deranged individual. No, he did not act alone. The killers are those politicians in high places who spout racist rhetoric, inciting hatred and bigotry. They rant that white people are now the "victims" who must "take back our country" from African Americans, Latinos, uppity women, gays and lesbians, poor people, and all the other folks fighting for dignity, equality, civil rights and civil liberties. These racist elements are open in their incitement of hatred of President Obama, our first African American president.

Among those murdered by the gunman was Reverend Clementa C. Pinckney, pastor of Mother Emanuel AME. Reverend Pinckney was also a South Carolina State

Senator who, a few weeks ago, delivered an impassioned speech on the Senate floor denouncing the shooting death of Walter Scott, fifty, an unarmed African American, by a white police officer in North Charleston. Scott was unarmed. He had been pulled over for having a broken tail light.

Reverend Pinckney's leadership in the struggle against police use of lethal force against innocent, unarmed African Americans, was likely the reason the racist killer targeted him for assassination.

Decades after I attended that Local 1199 strike rally, the union-busters struck again in Charleston. It was in 2001 and the target was the predominantly African American International Longshoremen's Association, Local 1422.

Dock workers peacefully picketing to win a decent contract were viciously assaulted by Charleston police and South Carolina troopers. Five were arrested and charged with incitement to riot. It was the beginning of a year-long nationwide struggle to "Free the Charleston Five."

Roy Rydell, himself a retired National Maritime Union seafarer, and I, traveled to Columbia, South Carolina to cover a massive rally at the state capitol building to demand freedom for the Charleston Five and a just settlement of the strike.

The labor movement mobilized a movement so strong that the shipping companies and union-busting forces were compelled to free the Charleston Five. I returned to Charleston for a victory rally at ILA Local 1422 headquarters, March 2, 2002.

In the spring of 2008, Reverend Pierre Williams and I rode a bus organized by the Black Caucus of the Maryland General Assembly down to Columbia to go door to door to help elect President Barack Obama, our first Black President. That struggle too, ended in victory.

There are lessons from these struggles. The labor movement, and all progressive forces, must unite against the racist hatemongers. We must organize solidarity rallies everywhere to express our outrage at this massacre. If the racists succeed in their scheme to divide us along lines of race, ethnicity, or gender, they will always win. If we are strong and united, we will always win.

President Obama greets sisters of James Byrd Jr. and mother of Matthew Shepard at White House after he signed Matthew Shepard and James Byrd, Jr. Hate Crimes Prevention Act Oct. 28, 2009. White House photo by Pete Souza

Grieving Sister: "Stand Up To Racism"
By Tim Wheeler

Feb. 23, 1999

Mary Verrett is still mourning the death of her brother, James Byrd Jr., the Black man dragged to his death behind a pickup truck by three white supremacists outside Jasper, Texas last June 7 in one of the most gruesome lynchings ever.

"We win and yet we still lose because we don't have him back," Verrett said moments after she listened in the courtroom to a jury find John William King guilty of first degree murder.

The jury, 11 whites and one African American, deliberated less than two-and-a-half hours to reach their verdict Feb. 22. Courtroom spectators applauded and

Byrd's family, including his children, wept. The jury is now deliberating whether to impose the death penalty or life imprisonment on King.

The *World* reached Mary Verrett by telephone at her family's home in Jasper where many of Byrd's friends and relations had gathered after the trial.

"This is a time for people to take a look at themselves and if they harbor prejudice, bigotry, racism and intolerance in their heart, they should make sure it does not lead to the kind of violence that took my brother's life," she said.

Byrd, described as a gentleman with a sweet singing voice, was walking home along a rural road when King and his accomplices, Shawn Berry, 24, and Lawrence Russell Brewer, 31, offered him a ride in the back of the pickup. They took him to a dirt-logging trail east of Jasper and brutally beat him.

They then chained him by his ankles to the bumper of the pickup and dragged him along a bumpy country road for three miles.

Dr. Tommy Brown, a pathologist, testified that Byrd was alive and conscious for two miles, propping himself on his elbows, despite the excruciating pain, to protect his head. When the pickup swerved to the left, Byrd's body swung to the right and his head and arm was torn off by a concrete drain pipe. King, an ex-convict, wears white supremacist body tattoos including a silhouette of a lynch victim hanging from a tree, Nazi-style SS lightening bolts and Aryan Nation proclamations.

According to trial testimony, King had told fellow inmates several years ago that he planned to "take out" a Black person to prove himself as a white supremacist. After his release from prison in 1997, King tried to start a Klan-like outfit called the Texas Rebel Soldiers Division of the Confederate Knights of the Ku Klux Klan.

While in jail, King sent a message to his accomplice, Lawrence Russell Brewer, that he had left his clothing spattered with Byrd's blood in his apartment. The message was intercepted and police found the damning evidence. King's cigarette lighter and a cigarette butt with his DNA on it were found at the site of the beating. In closing arguments, prosecutor Pat Hardy described the killers as "three robed riders coming straight out of hell. That's exactly what there was that night. After they dragged that poor man and tore his body to pieces, they dropped it right in front of a church and cemetery to show their defiance to God, to show their defiance of Christianity and everything that most people in this country stand for."

Jasper County District Attorney Guy James Gray told the jury that racism is like a virus. "It's something that's dangerous. It's something that spreads from one person to another," he said.

Verrette told the *World* she is well aware that the Klan and other hate organizations are active throughout the country. "He was just copying off other white supremacist groups and trying to organize his own," she said.

Law enforcement authorities, she said, "have these hate groups under close scrutiny. I realize that there is no legislation in the world that can command that we love one another or even like one another. But the legislators can and must stress that we all tolerate one another."

The Byrd lynching was a shocking wakeup call that racist violence as well as organized right wing vigilantism still festers throughout the nation.

A few months after the murder of Byrd came the brutal beating of Matthew Shepard of Wyoming, a gay student who was then tied to a fence in the freezing cold and left to die. There was also the case of Dr. Barnett Slepian, an abortion doctor, shot to death by an anti-abortion fanatic.

Many of the murders and brutalizations are committed by police officers - New York police, for example, who fired 41 bullets at Amadou Diallo, an unarmed, legal immigrant. He died from 19 bullet wounds. Yet to be tried and punished are the officers who brutalized Haitian immigrant Abner Louima.

Not forgotten is the bombing by white supremacists of the Oklahoma City federal building killing 168 men, women and children in April 1995.

NAACP President Kweisi Mfume said the verdict in the Byrd lynching "shouts across the world for the urgent need of this Congress to move quickly to strengthen and to pass anti-hate crime legislation."

Trial dates have not been set for the other two defendants.

Shipyard Strikers Defy Cop Beatings
By Tim Wheeler
Daily World

April 18, 1979
NEWPORT NEWS, VIRGINIA, APRIL 17—The militant Black and white shipbuilders of Steelworkers Local 8888 returned to their picket-lines today, bloodied but unbowed by the most brutal police attack on strikers in recent U.S. history.

Newport News police, reinforced by Virginia State Troopers rampaged along Washington Avenue yesterday, savagely beating peaceful pickets at the 37th St. and 50th St. gate of Tenneco Corporation's giant Newport News shipbuilding company. The attack was an attempt to crush the seven-week strike by United Steelworkers against Tenneco, owner of the two-mile long shipyard, the largest in the U.S.

More than seventy strikers were clubbed, over fifty were hospitalized, some with concussions, lacerated scalps and broken bones. At least two women were beaten, including a fourteen-year-old Black girl and a pregnant woman. Picketers as well as bystanders attempted to seek refuge from the police attack in restaurants that line the avenue, up and down the shipyard; but the police pursued them into the restaurants, dragging them out into the streets and beating them.

Scores were arrested, including Jack Hower, a steel union organizer who was later released on his own recognizance.

During the attack, a contingent of Newport News police marched to the 33rd St. headquarters of the United Steelworkers and, without warning or warrant, stormed the building, clubbing workers and their families who had gone to obtain strike benefits.

The attack began yesterday morning when more than 500 strikers marched to the shipyard gates, chanting, "88 close the gate," to confront scabs who have been crossing union picket lines. The police moved to break up the strikers' lines and, when the workers refused to move, attacked them. Most were charged with "assaulting police officers" and with violating the state's union-busting "right to work" law.

Wayne Crosby, president of the embattled union local, told the *Daily World* in an interview today, "What happened here yesterday reminds me of Nazi Germany. They put our union hall under siege. They came in here without a warning. They beat a fourteen-year-old girl who was here with her father to get strike benefits, and today she is on crutches. One of our union officers was beaten until the riot stick broke. He is in the hospital today with a concussion. Another striker has a broken leg."

As we talked in his cramped office, the telephone rang constantly with offers of help coming from union locals across the nation. Hundreds of workers, some of them with bandaged heads, waited in the jammed hallways of the strike headquarters. Hundreds more gathered on the sidewalk outside the union headquarters.

A telephone call came in for Crosby from the district director of the United Steelworkers in California, offering assistance to the heroic Newport News strikers. Crosby reported the events here, largely suppressed by the pro-corporate news media.

Crosby told the California union leaders, "The financial support is coming in good, keep it coming. That support is what is holding us together here. It shows us that we are not alone. Ask your locals to write to their congressmen and senators. Tell them to oppose shifting the Saratoga (an aircraft carrier) down here until Tenneco agrees to sit down and bargain with us."

Crosby added, "We don't think any company that violates the law, engages in strikebreaking, should get any government contracts."

Tenneco gets most of its business for its shipyard here from the U.S. Navy. Crosby said that Tenneco would come to terms with the union quickly if the federal government cut these contracts off.

Downtown Newport News was quiet today. But it had the uneasy calm of a war zone where at any moment a new spasm of police violence could be unleashed.

Postscript: Almost exactly 20 years later, I drove down to Newport News to cover another Local 8888 walkout. I remember the year that strike erupted because a friend gave me a T-shirt emblazoned with the slogan: "I WALKED THE LINE FOR 88 IN '99." They won that strike too.

A New Day In Birmingham
By Tim Wheeler

Nov. 15, 1979

BIRMINGHAM---For many years, Benjamin Davis' service station at the corner of 4th Ave. and 16th Street has been near the eye of the hurricane of struggle against racist oppression in this deep South steel city.

Two blocks away is the 16th Street Baptist Church, headquarters of Dr. Martin Luther King Jr.'s Birmingham Project during the 1960s when freedom riders faced the fire hoses, attack dogs, and electric cattle prods of police chief, T. Eugene "Bull" Connor. On Sept. 15, 1963, a bomb exploded in the church killing four children---Addie Mae Collins, Carol Robertson, Carol D. McNair, and Cynthia Wesley. It was a crime committed by the Ku Klux Klan with the connivance of the FBI.

During those years of martyrdom, Dr. King wrote his famous "Letter From A Birmingham Jail" branding the city as perhaps the "most segregated city in the nation." He said, "It was our faith that as Birmingham goes, so goes the South."

Mr. Davis lives with his wife, Sallye---herself a long-time civil rights activist----in a modest frame house at the top of a hill that also became a symbol of the struggle against racism. When Black families attempted to move

Richard Arrington who served 20 years as mayor of Birmingham. Photo courtesy of BlackPast.org

into the neighborhood, their newly purchased homes were destroyed in bomb blasts and the area became known as "Dynamite Hill." But the Davises were not easily intimidated and they stayed, rearing children, among them the eminent freedom fighter, Angela Yvonne Davis.

Mr. Davis who has lived with the struggle in Birmingham for 40 years, therefore spoke with satisfaction of the election, October 30, of Richard Arrington, a Black man, as mayor of Birmingham.

"I think it is quite an interesting thing to happen," he said in an interview with *World Magazine*. "Just a little more than 10 years ago, Blacks hardly had a chance to vote and now they have elected a Black man mayor of Alabama's largest city. This means there is going to be greater recognition of Black people, more respect for their rights."

The key to Arrington's stunning victory over Frank Parsons, a millionaire businessman, a George Wallace supporter, who ran a law and order fear campaign, was building a powerful interracial grassroots coalition of voters. Arrington took 98-99% of the Black vote and nearly 15% of the white vote as he attacked the racist polarization tactics of his opponent.

When the votes were counted, it was 44,798 votes---or 51.1%---for Arrington to 42,814 votes----or 48.9%----for Parsons. Arrington carried by overwhelming votes, every Black district in the city. Arrington cut significantly into the bi-racial 35th District and split the 36th District 959 for Parsons and 888 for Arrington.

Parsons carried the almost all-white 32nd District with 7,464 votes but Arrington garnered 2,154 votes for himself. These votes in districts Arrington lost added up to the swing white vote which combined with a solid Black vote to produce Arrington's victory. Parsons was not able to cut into a single predominantly Black district to offset Arrington's advantage.

"The Klan elements are reeling from this election," said Scott Douglas, a Black community activist in Birmingham. He pointed out that in the months leading up to the election, the Klan had unleashed a determined racist offensive which included marches and rallies in Birmingham, Decatur, and other Alabama towns and cities. The Klan had seized on the legal lynch trial of Tommy Lee Hines, a retarded Black youth arrested on rape charges, to spread a campaign of terrorism which included dragging a Black man into the woods and severely beating him.

In Birmingham itself, a white fireman, trading on the publicity around the so-called "Weber" Supreme Court "reverse discrimination" case, filed a lawsuit against an affirmative action program intended to increase Black hiring and promotion in the Birmingham Fire Department. Birmingham's 275,000 population is 54% Black but its 700-member police force is over 90% white with a sordid record of vicious brutality against the Black population.

On June 29, George Sands, a white cop with a record of more than 15 complaints of police brutality, shot in cold blood a young Black woman named Bonita Carter as she sat in her car outside a convenience store. Instead of firing Sands and seeking his prosecution for murder, Mayor David Vann reassigned Sands and appointed a citizen "fact-finding commission."

This white-wash touched off an angry outcry. The Southern Christian Leadership Conference called for a mass protest march. More than 4,000 showed up, the largest mass protest in Birmingham since the 1960s.

Against this backdrop, Arrington, son of a sharecropper, a doctor of zoology, an eight-year veteran on the Birmingham City Council, denounced the cover-up and murder of Ms. Carter and announced he would run for mayor. Mayor Vann had refused to release the name of the killer cop. Arrington made the cop's identity known as well as his long r4ecord of brutality against other Black citizens of this city.

Arrington ran in the first round, October 9, without the backing of prominent Black political leaders in Birmingham. They endorsed Vann based on his past record as a civil rights attorney who had argued the "one man, one vote case before the Supreme Court. It was also believed that a Black man could not win an election in Birmingham and that even running a Black candidate risked helping the election of a racist candidate.

But in a display of independence that confounded all the predictions, Black voters flocked to Arrington's banners. He won the first round with 44% of the vote compared to 16.9% for Parsons, his nearest contender. Vann ran a distant third with only 15.9% of the vote. A Ku Klux Klansman who ran for mayor received less than 2% of the vote.

Said Scott Douglas, "This is a striking victory for electoral independence in Alabama. The voters, in selecting Arrington for the runoff, went against the advice of the mainline Democratic Party in the Black community."

The Jefferson County Progressive Democrats, tied to the Alabama Democratic Council, had endorsed Vann on the basis of a "lesser of evils" outlook, Douglass added. But voters rejected this and displayed a determination to elect a genuinely independent, progressive alternative.

"This is a contribution to democracy for the entire state of Alabama and the South," Douglas continued. "It will definitely give encouragement not just to Blacks alone but to workers and to women running for office."

Birmingham has undergone a deep-going economic shift in the past decade. Standing at the top of Red Mountain is a statue of Vulcan, Roman God of the Forge, symbolizing vast deposits of coal, iron, and limestone that supply the steel mills of the city. Republic Steel however, closed its mill here several years ago, and U.S. Steel is threatening to curtail or closer its aging Fairfield works.

Meanwhile, the University of Alabama at Birmingham has established a prestigious medical center here and together with other hospitals more than 8,500 medical workers live in the area. Thus, steel workers, coal miners and medical workers form the backbone of the working class in the city.

Tyrone Tolbert, a young Black man who served as Arrington's volunteer media coordinator spoke to World Magazine at Arrington's headquarters in downtown Birmingham a few days before the runoff. Telephones rang persistently, canvassers hurried in and out and a crew of Black and white volunteers sat at tables stuffing envelopes with literature urging Arrington's election.

"Arrington has kept in close touch with the people as you can see by the numbers of volunteers we have," he said. "He has worked his entire political career against the politics of polarization. He is a mayor for all the people. He is the one candidate who came out and spoke against brutality in any fork. There is no excuse, when the people are paying the police with their tax dollars, for the police to be out of control."

Vann, he said, frittered away the strong support he had among Black voters when he attempted to evade the Carter murder case. "By setting up this so-called citizen's commission, he opened the door for Sands to get away with what he had done---and now Sands has filed for 'disability pay,' claiming he is no longer able to function!" Tolbert said.

The issue of "human dignity, human rights," cannot be compromised in this manner, he added. "I don't care how good Vann's record was in the past. When a politician forgets his constituency, it's time to call him to reckoning."

The times have changed, he continued, and the "standards" for what constitutes a forthright stand against racism are therefore higher. "More than liberalism is involved here. It's a question of who can deliver."

Arrington's victory, he said, was the fruit of a tremendous grassroots outpouring from the Black community. "He had students from Miles College, the University of Alabama at Birmingham, by the hundreds volunteering to do work.....And Arrington, himself, did a tremendous amount of door-to-door canvassing. He had a good cross-section. Over in the Greenspring area, we had a headquarters staffed mostly by white volunteers," he said.

The atmosphere at Parson's headquarters just down the street was a stunning contrast. First of all, it was practically deserted. The half dozen people present were all white. William Campbell, Parsons' campaign coordinator, was able to name only one Black person who had endorsed Parsons' election. Campbell said the issue in the campaign was "allegations against the police that have been proven false." He argued, "We won't be able to build the morale of the police as long as the people keep hollering peace brutality."

In the final week of the campaign, in desperation. Parsons' supporters ran thinly veiled racist newspaper advertisements headlined, "A Tale of Two Cities," falsely warning that Birmingham would become like Atlanta, "murder capital of the U.S." if the city followed Atlanta's lead and elected a Black mayor.

But this attempt to polarize the white vote backfired. The Birmingham Labor Council endorsed Arrington. J.H. Goggans, a member of the BLC screening committee told World Magazine each of the candidates had been given 30 minutes to present his case. "The Birmingham Labor Council is a majority white and I think if they had seen this as a racial issue, they would not have endorsed Arrington," he said. "But we did not judge them on race. We judged them on merit, what they would do for labor, to create more jobs, better housing. Arrington won."

The endorsement brought with it the backing of Birmingham's 9,000 member United Steelworkers Union as well as the backing of the 8,500 hospital workers. However, the Central Alabama Building Trades Council top leadership, reflecting racist and class collaborationism, voted unanimously to endorse Parsons.

Postscript: In the very hot summer of 1984, I was back in Birmingham, this time not with a reporter's pen and pad but with a petition clipboard. I was one of about 20 stalwarts collecting signatures to place Gus Hall and Angela Davis on the ballot in Alabama for President and Vice President of the United States. A slim, handsome African American man approached me. He looked vaguely familiar as I launched into my pitch in praise of Hall and Davis. He listened politely. Then he took my pen and wrote his name: "Benjamin Davis." With the help of Angela Davis' dad, she and Gus Hall won ballot status in Alabama and received 4,671 votes, enough, in my estimation, to make Angela Alabama's "favorite daughter."

Thousands March in Virginia for ERA
By Tim Wheeler
Daily World

January 15, 1980

RICHMOND, VIRGINIA, JANUARY 14—Led by Newport News shipyard workers of Steelworkers' Local 8888, thousands of trade unionists marched on the Virginia state capital here Sunday, chanting "Equal rights, equal pay, ratify ERA."

The demonstration to demand that the Virginia legislature end its maneuvering and approve the Equal Rights Amendment (ERA) for women drew busloads of protesters from Detroit, Cleveland, Pittsburgh, New York City, Philadelphia, Baltimore, Washington D.C., and Raleigh, North Carolina. Thousands of the protesters came from towns and cities throughout Virginia. Contingents also came from as far away as California and Texas. The action was sponsored by the Virginia Labor for Equal Rights Now, the state AFL-CIO, the United Auto Workers, the Coalition of Black Trade Unionists, the Coalition of Labor Union Women, the Southern Christian Leadership Conference, the National Organization of Women, teachers unions and many others.

Virginia is a crucial state in the drive for ratification of the constitutional amendment, which is three states short of the two-thirds majority needed.

The march streamed down Franklin Street from the assembly point towards the Virginia capital building on a raw January day. The protesters carried banners that read: "Women make 59¢ for every dollar a man makes— we need the ERA." and "Women hold up half the sky," and "Tidewater labor says pass the ERA."

Massive contingents of steelworkers from Pittsburgh, Detroit, Baltimore, and Newport News spearheaded the march, followed by delegations of hundreds of electrical worker who belonged to the United Electrical, Radio and Machine Workers International Union. Over 1,000 teachers marched under the banner of the Virginia and Maryland National Education Association. Members of the American Federation of Teachers were also present. United Auto Workers members from New Jersey and Pennsylvania made a vast contingent. Hundreds marched under the banner of the United Food and Commercial Workers Union, including a large contingent of New York City Meatcutters. International Association of Machinists and the Communication Workers of America also added large contingents.

A contingent of women coal miners, members of the United Mine Workers from western Pennsylvania and from Oakridge, Tennessee, drew applause as they marched with banners. One placard carried by a group of Mormons declared "You cannot excommunicate equality—Mormons for the ERA."

Leading this group was Sonya Johnson, expelled from the Church of Latter Day Saints in a rightwing gang-up spearheaded by a Mormon bishop who is personnel director of the CIA. Ms. Johnson told the *Daily World*, "I'm here with many other Mormons to demand the Virginia legislature approve the ERA."

She said she has received 6,000 messages in support since her expulsion. Ms. Johnson received a heroine's welcome when she spoke to the vast throng in the state's capital, laid out by Thomas Jefferson in 1787. "The new right is losing momentum as we gain momentum," 'she said.

Addie Wyatt, the vice president of United Food and Commercial Workers, and a leader of the Coalition of Black

Trade Unionists, drew thunderous applause when she quoted a famous speech "I AM A Woman" by Sojourner Truth. She declared, "We are here today as men and women to confirm the fact that this nation has more than 110 million women who want to be free as much as their brothers are free. The time is now to ratify the ERA."

Men, she added, must become equal partners in the struggle to end "discrimination, exploitation, and oppression of women."

She added, "Some people go through life wondering what is happening . . . and some people go through life making things happen. We are here to make things happen."

Joseph E. Lowery, president of the Southern Christian Leadership Conference, charged that Dr. Martin Luther King was murdered by those who oppress women, labor, and Blacks."

The decade of the 1970s was marked by attempts of government and big business to take away gains people had made in economic and social well-being. He blasted the Carter Administration's hysteria over the U.S. hostages held in Iran, declaring, "We want those hostages released but we want the release of the hostages right here in America—the women, the Black folks, labor, held hostage from their equal rights.

"If we want to make the 80's better than the 70's then we better get together. It's time for all God's children to rise up."

Eleanor Smeal, president of NOW, told the crowd, "This is an economic movement. Thank God the women's movement, the labor movement, the Black civil rights movement, is united. We are not going to let the "new right" march us back to the 1800s. Our daughters are not going to put up with .59¢ on the dollar. Virginia, wake up, ratify the ERA."

John Kennedy, president of District 28 of the United Mine Workers of America, said, "Miners are fighting people. They don't roll over and play dead. We thank you for the support you gave the mineworkers in the 1978 strike. We are interested in equal rights for every working person in this country, whether they be man or woman, Black or white."

Don't Sleep with JP Stevens

Daily World

This is the second of four articles on the victory of the workers in organizing a union at J.P. Stevens.

By Tim Wheeler

October 29, 1980

ROANOKE RAPIDS, NORTH CAROLINA OCTOBER 27—In the J.P. Stevens company bag of union-busting tricks, racism was the most dangerous threat to union victory according to Black and white workers here still celebrating their first union contract with the "corporation outlaw."

Clyde Bush, staff director of the Amalgamated Clothing and Textile Workers Union (ACTWU), told the *Daily World* that the union would have been defeated if the workers, sixty percent white and forty percent Black, had succumbed to the company's divide and conquer game plan.

"The company tried every way it could to divide the workers along racial lines," Bush said in an interview at ACTWU's storefront office in this small southern mill town.

Company lies

"J.P. Stevens used a few pro-company people out on the shop floor to spread the story that it was going to be a 'Black union'," Bush said. "If the union gets in, they said, all the Blacks are going to be promoted. You won't be able to bid on jobs."

The real aim was to foment racial discord, he said, as a part of the company's drive for a decertification election. Just how touch and go it was is revealed by the result of the second National Labor Relations Board election, August 28, 1974.

Of 3,205 workers who voted at seven plants in Roanoke Rapids, 1,688 voted for the union and 1,448 voted against. A switch of only 100 votes would have meant defeat for the ACTWU.

Bush said the union fought the company lies at each monthly union meeting. "I stressed very hard that this is a union for all Stevens workers," he said.

J.P. Stevens has practiced, profitable, highly institutionalized racist discrimination at its eighty-five plants employing 44,000 workers ever since it moved its operations South during the 1950s looking for cheap labor.

In 1963, a white Stevens truck driver earning $3.35 an hour left for a better job. Robert Mallory, a Black worker, replaced him but was paid only $2.35 per hour. "I asked why I couldn't get the same thing the white man was getting," said Mallory in a widely distributed ACTWU leaflet. "I never got an answer whatsoever from any of them."

In a suit against the company, Mallory charged he was not only paid lower wages, but he worked harder. The white worker transported five trailers while he delivered thirteen, more than doubling production. Mallory's suit is still pending in the North Carolina courts.

Ruling against Stevens

On January 24, 1977, the U.S. Forth Circuit Court of Appeals issued a broad ruling charging J.P. Stevens with violation of Title VII of the U.S. Civil Rights Act. The ruling came in a case brought by A.C. Sherrill.

Sherrill, a Black worker at Stevens Stanley, North Carolina, plant, accused the company of harassing him and five other Black workers so mercilessly they were forced to quit.

Stevens was seeking to punish the Black workers for having complained to the) against Stevens racist job practices. The court ordered the workers reinstated and also directed J.P. Stevens to provide promotional opportunities for the Black workers.

Bennett Taylor, thirty-eight, a member of the ACTWU's Roanoke Rapids Bargaining Committee, said racist discrimination is still being practiced at the J.P., Stevens plants.

"Even now, Black workers are concentrated in the warehouse which is paid on a lower wage scale," Taylor, who is Black, charged in an interview with this reporter.

Warehouse hiring

"In the fabricating department where I work all the warehouse workers are Black except one and he is a truck driver and is paid a better wage. Whites might start out in the warehouse but they are transferred out immediately," he said.

Taylor said the bargaining committee knows that the union must wage a continuing struggle to root out the discriminatory system first because justice demands it. At the same time, he continued, the very existence of the union depends on the unity of Black and white based on job equality.

That's why, he explained, one of the key demands by the bargaining committee was for an end to the system of departmental seniority in favor of plant-wide seniority. This demand, he said, was one in the recently ratified contract.

He pointed out that J.P. Stevens had used the departmental seniority system not only to impose lower wages on Black workers but also force them to bear the brunt of layoffs.

"If the company intends to live up to the contract, posting all jobs, open bidding, plant-wide seniority it will make a difference in stopping the discrimination," Taylor continued.

"We couldn't keep our mouths shut during the six years of negotiations. We kept our members up to date on the battle. The bargaining committee felt responsible because the people in the plants had elected us to represent them."

Reverend speaks out

Reverend Edward Fleming, a Black minister who has been a staunch supporter of the Stevens workers, told the *Daily World* in an interview that the company exploited the fact that Black workers rallied so quickly and in such numbers to the union.

This, he said, was the origin of the company line that the union would be "Black." Reverend Fleming, a twenty-three-year veteran of labor in the Stevens plant, was one of many Black workers fired and blacklisted for his pro-union activities.

"I was fired after I started speaking out in my sermons. I told my congregation that the poor needed to be organized," Fleming said in an interview at his modest home outside Roanoke Rapids.

He said the most significant factor in the victory was the union's success in convincing white workers to join with their Black brothers and sisters in the struggle for a union.

Major breakthrough

"This is a major breakthrough as far as organizing North Carolina is concerned," he said. "It will help in organizing South Carolina, Georgia and Alabama—wherever employers attempt to pit white workers against Black workers."

The workers at J.P. Stevens, he continued, "will be working under a union contract. It is going to mean the company has got rules to go by. There can be no favoritism.

"I have known supervisors who would let a white worker show up ten minutes late but if a Black worker did the same thing, he would be written up or even dismissed, especially if he supported the union. They harassed me every time I showed up a minute late," he said.

Reverend Fleming said the support of the Black community in the Roanoke Rapids area was crucial to the victory. "The union met at the First Baptist Church in Roanoke Rapids because a Black church was the only place open to them. Black workers were the ones who started this whole thing. The community supported them but it was the workers themselves that took the lead."

Joyce Bush, who worked as a weaver for fourteen years at J.P. Stevens until she became a full-time volunteer for the union, told the *Daily World* that she was one of many hundreds of white workers who rejected the company line that the "union is Black."

During an interview interrupted by the constant ringing of the telephone and by a procession of workers coming into the union hall to sign their dues check-off card, she told the *Daily World* how she had come to the union.

"I come from a union family," she said. "My step-father was a shop steward. He was a member of the International Brotherhood of Electrical Workers, so I knew what a union could do for us.

"When I first started to work, it was mostly Black workers that joined the union. The company spread the word around 'you'll get fired if you join the union.'

"But one day a bunch of us just decided to put union buttons on at the beginning of the second shift. About three-fourths of us did and all the boss could do was give us dirty looks. I became very active distributing union literature and here I am now working as a union volunteer."

Update: A few weeks after J.P. Stevens workers won this historic victory, J.P. Stevens went out of

business and closed all it's factories. It showed just how ruthless Wall Street banks and corporations are in their drive to destroy unions, drive workers' wages and benefits to starvation levels.

Union Pride at Delta Pride
People's Daily World

November 6, 1986

INDIANOLA, MISSISSIPPI—Employees of Delta Pride, a catfish processing firm here, struck a blow for human dignity October 10 when they voted 489-346 to join the United Food and Commercial Workers, AFL-CIO.

The workers, 95% young Afro-American women, have endured years of sex harassment, arbitrary dismissal, and wages barely over the minimum wage at the sprawling fish packing plant outside this Mississippi Delta town, where unemployment is above 20%.

The lavatories at the plant had no doors and male supervisors routinely violated the privacy of the women workers.

With cotton, soybean and other cash crops at rock bottom prices, hundreds of farmers are digging ponds and stocking them with catfish. Catfish production has become a $650 million industry, one of the fastest growing in the state. The processing plants where the catfish are cleaned, fileted, frozen and packaged employ 4,000 workers with a payroll of more than $40 million.

The American Catfish Institute has launched a $6 million media campaign to promote catfish consumption across the nation.

Members of the newly formed Delta Pride unit of UFCW—now the biggest union shop in the Mississippi Delta—convened a membership meeting one recent evening at the headquarters of United Steelworkers Local 8421 in Indianola.

Doug Coutee, a field representative of the UFCW, read to the crowd from the Congressional Record a speech delivered on the House floor by Representative Charles

Hayes (D-ILL.,) a former international president of the UFCW. Hayes' speech hailed the vote by Delta Pride workers as a "historic victory" for human rights in a stronghold of anti-unionism.

David Day, a negotiator for the UFCW assigned to the newly formed unit, affiliated with the Memphis-based UFCW Local 1529, warned the workers that Delta Pride has not given up. The company, he said, is still maneuvering with appeals to the National Labor Relations Board to have their vote annulled. When Delta Pride exhausts their appeals, "we will ask for a meeting to begin negotiating a contract," he said.

Mary Young, a Delta Pride employee for three and a half years and the mother of three young children, spearheaded the drive.

"It was the treatment we got, the low wages and no benefits that made up our minds to join the union," Young said. Speedup in the plant is ferocious, she said, with each worker expected to process 800 pounds of fish daily. Blood and guts fly. A bandsaw cuts off fish heads and several women have lost fingers in the unshielded blades. The women on the strip table filet the fish with razor sharp knives; vicious cuts are a daily hazard.

Her husband is a member of Local 8421 of the United Steelworkers of America, which represents the 500 workers at Modern Line, a firm that processes lawn mowers and other equipment in Indianola. Many of the Delta Pride workers are married to Modern Line workers, and Local 8421 played a critical support role in the UFCW victory. Indeed, a coalition of unions, churches, and civil rights groups sprang up in solidarity with the workers.

Dorothy McDaniel, a shy, quiet-spoken woman who has worked nearly two years fileting catfish, displayed the scar that traces along the back of her hand. "It took fifty stitches to close it," she said. "The girl who was working beside me, her knife slipped and cut my hand. They won't even take us to the doctor when we get cut. We have to clock out. We don't get paid while we're getting treated. And if you don't come back to work the next day, they fire you. We get cuts every day.

"I went to work straight out of high school," she continued. "It's about the only job available around here. I asked my supervisor to be moved from the strip table. He told me if I wanted to move, I can move on right out the door.

"To me, the most important thing is a raise. I'm single. I can't live on $3.80 an hour. I need more money."

Effie Lewis works in the department that freezes the fish with carbon dioxide, "dry ice." Her first job was with Fishland, another catfish company. "You have to work so fast," she said. "And since we voted for the union, they are really getting down on us. Rough talk. Switching us from job to job. They keep us late. They're trying to wear us down."

Toyah Webb, who has worked as a skinner since March 20, described the panic among the supervisors when the company got wind of the organizing drive. "They gave us a pay raise right away," she said, chuckling with delight. "They raised my pay from $3.45 to $3.80, a thirty-five cent raise. But it didn't change my mind at all. I knew the union could do better. I knew it was just to try to keep me from voting for the union. I had my mind made up. I have three children. I need more than $3.80 an hour."

Mary Young said she was moved to launch the union drive when she and several others received a questionnaire in the mail from UFCW. Last January 25, a UFCW field organizer met with her and two others. The next day after work, the three workers were in the parking lots and on the streets of Indianola urging their fellow workers to sign.

"Right off the bat, the company called a big meeting with us, telling us is we signed the cards we could lose our jobs, the plant would close. On January 28, two people who were active in the campaign got fired. They were trying to find out who was passing the cards. They'd fire them right away."

She said a complaint was filed asking the court to order these workers rehired with back pay. "Job security is one of the main issues. They fire you after two days, two weeks, two years, for nothing. And we have nothing to say about it."

Ploys used by Delta Pride to frighten its employees were described by Doug Coutee. Charles Evers, the pro-corporate mayor of Fayette, Mississippi, was brought into the Delta Pride plant to urge the women to vote no. The firm even arranged for another catfish processor, Pride of the Pond, where workers had voted earlier 60-10 for UFCW recognition, to stage a fraudulent shutdown on the eve of the vote to scare the Delta Pride workers.

"But some of the workers from that plant came down and told us it was a bunch of baloney," Coutee said. "The day after we won our victory, the plant reopened. It was just an attempt to intimidate the workers."

Coutee, a native of the state, said the Delta Pride vote is probably the biggest victory for trade unionism in the history of the Mississippi Delta.

"I think you will see the fear go away," he said. "You'll see it removed as the union progresses, as these workers get a contract, as their economic situation improves. It shows that with a union, they can stand up and fight for themselves."

He said, "People are already becoming totally involved in their communities, whether it be civil rights, political action, or moving on to organize more plants in the delta. You could just see so much happiness that night, October 10, when the vote was counted at Delta Pride. People were crying with joy because they had never witnessed anything like this before."

Mary Young, wearing a pin with the words "Union for Concerned Women," playing on the union's initials, also commented on the upsurge of activity and the new sense of "union pride at Delta Pride."

"A couple of months ago," she said, "we had a school boycott to demand that a Black school superintendent be appointed in Indianola. The children are Black. Why shouldn't we have a Black superintendent. We won. Then we won our election at Delta Pride.

"Now we're working to elect Mike Epsy to Congress, the first Black person from this district in more than 100 years."

Epsy, the young Black deputy district attorney of Mississippi who was campaigning against a Reaganite Republican, spoke at several solidarity rallies in Indianola.

"Why did all this start happening right now? We're Black women, most of us single parents. There is no other income we can fall back on if we lose these jobs. Those like myself, who have husbands, can't make it without that second income.

"Finally we woke up. We just got tired of being walked all over, worked to death. We are fighting for our dignity. That's what the union is all about."

Fighting for Their Land
People's Daily World

September 11, 1986
SUMTER, SOUTH CAROLINA—Frank Martin stood in his drought-stricken field holding a handful of stunted ears of corn. "Last year my yield was 130 bushels per acre," he said. "This year I estimate it will be fourteen bushels per acre."

The cornstalks, usually taller than a man and emerald green, are only waist-high and burnt a sickly brown. Weeks of scorching drought this summer forced Secretary of Agriculture Richard E. Lyng to declare most of South Carolina a disaster area. Rain finally came two weeks ago—too late to save the crops. Sumter County is among the hardest hit, and the farmers here presumably qualify for Farmers Home Administration (FmHA) loans at five percent interest up to $100,000.

Afro-American farmers like Frank Martin have a need for disaster aid unequalled among tillers in this region. Yet several Afro-American farmers reported they have received no help from the Reagan administration. Some said they have faced years of rejection or stalling of their applications for FmHA crop loans. Loans that are approved are smaller than those granted their white counterparts.

Denial of those loans means farmers cannot purchase seed and fertilizer to plant their crops. It is coupled with the Reagan administration's policy of forcing down the price of cash crops below the price of production.

In 1910, Black farmers owned over fifteen million acres in the South. By 1970, it had been slashed to less than six million acres. According to the Census of Agriculture, minority farmers in South Carolina owned 1,068,655 acres in 1950. By 1978 that had been whittled to 297,640 acres—a seventy-two percent decline.

"So many white and Black farmers have gone bankrupt in Sumter County that FmHA is holding tens of thousands of foreclosed acres. Mac McCloud, the owner of Piggly Wiggly stores—one of the biggest supermarkets chains in the South—recently bought 7,000 acres of foreclosed land in Sumter County from FmHA. "I think we're going to get to the point eventually where the large companies control our food production. It looks to me like we're in for a long-term disaster," he said.

Martin and his neighbors have begun to fight back. He took this reporter to a meeting of the Mideastern Concerned Needy Farmers Association (MCNFA) at Emmanuel United Methodist Church in the town of Sumter.

The sixty farmers—Black and white—adopted by-laws for their newly founded organization and planned participation in this weekend's United Farmers and Ranchers Congress in St. Louis. An integrated delegation of thirty or more South Carolina farmers will attend the giant meeting.

Leon Walker Sr., a lifelong farmer, told the meeting he had been approved for FmHA loans in 1980 and 1982. "I looked at my check on the counter in 1980 and again in 1982, and Mr. Paul Booth (Sumter County FmHA director) refused to give them to me," declared Walker, who is Afro-American. "I couldn't understand why he did it when the county committee had approved me and the check had been sent down from Washington. I've had two children in college for six straight years and you know it's been hard."

Walker assailed FmHA for turning over to private bill collection agencies, last week, delinquent FmHA loans held by 6,000 debt-stricken farmers totaling $630 million. "They are sending out letters demanding immediate payment," Walker said. The Reverend O.S. Scott, president of MCNFA, said, "Many farmers here in Sumter County, both Black and white, will lose their homes, their farms, all they've worked for if they are not able to cover their FmHA note. Those individuals are in desperate shape. It is an emergency. Nothing has been received from the federal government in drought assistance for the farmers here."

Last month, the National Council of Churches in New York sent a $10,000 check for the MCNFA farmers. Last week a church in Pennsylvania sent one semi-truckload of hay from the much publicized "haylift." Scott said each of the neediest MCNFA farmers received $400 and a few bales of hay to keep their cattle, horses and mules alive—although hogs eat grain, not hay.

As appreciated as this private assistance is, he said, it barely scratches the surface of the need.

"We need hundreds of thousands of dollars in assistance today," Reverend Scott said.

Leon Crump, field organizer for the Federation of Southern Cooperatives Land Assistance Fund (FSC-LAF) urged the farmers to take their grievances to St. Louis "so that your concerns can be a part of a national movement of farmers."

Crump said his organization is fighting to defend all family farmers, with special emphasis on preserving Black-owned land. He circulated a resolution adopted at the annual meeting of FSC-LAF, August 15, calling for a two-year moratorium on all government and private bank foreclosures; emergency grants rather than loans to drought-stricken and debt-stricken farmers; PARITY prices set at ninety percent for all crops; special assistance to "limited resource" farmers, etcetera.

The resolution also calls for affirmative action to increase Black and other minority management of the Department of Agriculture, FmHA, and other government agencies.

The resolution calls on farmers to "work together, form coalitions, pool resources" to defend their farms.

Scattered among the participants at the MCNFA meeting were several young farmers. One of them is Connie Walker, assistant secretary of the new organization. Walker (no relation to Leon Walker, Senior,) told this reporter she and her husband are fighting to hold on to their 400-acre farm.

"I guess we're about the youngest farmers here," she said. "We're trying to make it as full-time farmers. We have two girls—five and fourteen. It's hard when you don't have any money. You try to provide the children with clothes and school supplies, try to pay the doctor's bills."

Tim Newman, thirty-two, is one of several white farmers who have joined the MCNFA. "I love farming," he said. "My dad farmed for sixty years before me. My wife and I want to step in and carry it on. But I'm making plans to get a fulltime job. It's a shame when you can't make a living farming. It's the end of the American way of life."

Women Lawmakers' Bill Compensates Black Farmers
People's Weekly World

Sept. 24, 2010

WASHINGTON—With Black farmers applauding during a September 23 rally on the Capitol grounds, Senators Kay Hagen of North Carolina and Blanche Lincoln of Arkansas, both Democrats, unveiled their bill to provide $1.25 billion to compensate African American farmers for decades of discrimination by the U.S. Department of Agriculture (USDA).

The open-air rally came at the end of a march by Black farmers and their families from USDA to Capitol Hill. The protesters walked behind a tractor driven by John Boyd, president of the National Black Farmers Association (NBFA). They carried a big banner, "Black Farmers Demand Justice."

Senator Hagen told the crowd, "Since I came to the Senate, I have been working tirelessly to rectify this injustice. Over 4,000 African American farmers in my state of North Carolina and 75,000 across the country are waiting for their settlement. Unfortunately, the Congress has failed to live up to its obligations."

Hagen, joined by Senators Lincoln and Mary Landrieu (D-LA), today introduced a freestanding bill to fund the $1.25 billion settlement authored by President Obama and approved in a House-funding bill in August.

Funding for the settlement was also attached to a Senate spending bill but was dropped at the last minute in the face of Republican opposition. The only Republican who has endorsed the Hagan-Lincoln-Landrieu bill is Iowa Senator Charles Grassley.

Senator Lincoln said, "It is way past the time we passed this. We know what the issue is. We need to get the resources to these farmers." Tens of thousands have already lost their farms due to discrimination in granting federal crop loans that are routinely approved for white farmers.

Lincoln said Congress must also extend the statute of limitations used to deny benefits to Black farmers who missed the deadline to apply for the so-called Pigford lawsuit upheld by a federal judge. She also called for creation of a civil rights office in the Agriculture Department. "We need to make sure that discrimination in the USDA is gone."

Representative Barbara Lee (D-CA), chairwoman of the Congressional Black Caucus (CBC), said that the opponents of the settlement always argue it will swell the federal deficit, "and yet we found the money to fund two wars and tax cuts for the wealthy. This has exacerbated an economic catastrophe for Black farmers. The time to correct this injustice is now."

Representative Sheila Jackson Lee (D-TX) said she has "walked the walk" in rural Texas and seen Black farmers "scratching out a living, helping feed America, and these farmers could not get assistance from their own Agriculture Department. We are waiting for someone on the Republican side, someone from the 'Party of NO' to help deliver justice."

Boyd, who operates a small farm in Virginia, told the rally he drove his tractor, renamed "Justice" to Capitol Hill today as he has every day so far in September. "I will keep on driving it up here until justice is done. The Black farmers are dying," he said. "This loss and this discrimination is real. It breaks down lives, tears apart families. We want this bill passed now!"

He thanked the Congressional Black Caucus for pushing the $1.25 billion settlement through the House. He also thanked Obama for introducing a bill to compensate farmers when he was a Senator from Illinois. "And we thank President Obama for reaching this really historic settlement. For years I walked the corridors in Washington and it did not happen under President Bush." The crowd applauded. Boyd told the *World*, "I'm very hopeful the Senate will act on this in September." Senate Majority Leader Harry Reid, "said he will try to move it," Boyd added. "We need two Republican Senators. So far we have one, Chuck Grassley of Iowa."

Hamlet, N.C.: The Day Their World Caught Fire
People's Weekly World
By Tim Wheeler

September 28, 1991

HAMLET,NORTH CAROLINA—Liesha Turner remembers that moment when someone screamed "fire" and

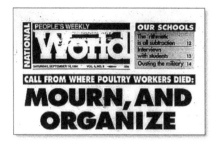

she turned and saw flames and smoke billowing from the chicken fryer a few steps from where she was working on the marinade line.

She is one of the survivors of the September 3 fire that killed twenty-five poultry workers and injured eighty-six at the non-union Imperial Foods Products plant across the railroad tracks from this picturesque town in North Carolina's Piedmont region. She and another survivor, Ella Mae McBride, took me on a guided tour around the outside of the windowless brick plant one recent afternoon. "It was like a wall of fire coming toward me," Turner said. "I started running toward the back of the plant. But we got stuck at the back door. Everyone was banging on the door. They were packed down in the hole where the back door is. I turned and ran out another door. I fell and injured my leg and back. I could hear people inside screaming, "Let me out.' Then there was an explosion. When they finally opened that door, the bodies fell out. They brought them out one-by-one and laid them together right here on the grass."

She pointed out the fire-blackened bricks around the doors that had been locked during the fire. The stench of rotting chicken was heavy in the air. "I hope a lot will come out of this," said Turner. "A lot of people were killed, including my cousin, Rosa Chambers. We are all mourning. Grandma is really taking it hard. This was no accident. It wasn't an accident that they kept the fire doors locked. I think the company is responsible."

The dead have been buried, the funerals and memorial services completed. Hamlet, population 6,000, is now struggling to bind up its wounds and bring life back into a semblance of normalcy.

In 1990 Hamlet won the designation, "All American City." The lawns here were well manicured. Most of the houses are neatly painted. The public housing units where many of the Imperial workers live are immaculate. Main Street is lined with beautifully maintained storefronts that could make it a setting for a "Bonnie and Clyde" period-piece movie. The CSX Seaboard railroad runs through town and each October there is a "Seaboard Festival" that brings 5,000 or more to celebrate.

"It's a town that takes a lot of pride in itself," said Reverend Harold Miller of the First Baptist Church, president of the Hamlet Ministerial Association, during an interview in his office. Reverend Miller has devoted twelve to sixteen hours daily since the disaster to comfort the families and arrange for victim assistance.

"There was a struggle to refurbish the library. Over $100,000 was raised through Tupperware parties, bake sales, that sort of thing. When the hospital was in trouble, the community rallied again to keep it open. And during this tragedy, again, people responded. In a town as small as this, when one of us is hurting, all of us hurt."

Of those who died, eighteen were young African-American women. They left behind forty-two school-age children. In most cases fathers, grandparents, aunts and uncles have stepped forward to care for the motherless children. One of them is Peggy Brown, whose sister, Mary Quick, died in the blaze, leaving three children. "All my children are grown but I have two grandchildren who are living with me," Brown told me. "Ironically, I had to purchase a larger house to make room for my grandchildren. It worked out that we were fortunate enough to have a place to provide a home for Mary's children. I know it is what she would have wanted."

There is much trauma and the school system is trying to help these children cope with their loss. But Reverend Miller warned that many problems of adjustment stretch into the future. "When so many mothers die, it means the loss will be with us for generations," he said.

Reverend Miller had high praise for the AFL-CIO, which sent organizers to assist the families. "Labor has been a big help," he said. "They have contributed not only their moral strength. They also provided new clothing. They have helped out with fuel expenses so relatives could visit survivors who are recovering in the hospital. I have been very impressed."

Reverend Miller assailed Emmet and Bradley Roe, the Georgia-based owners of Imperial Food Products. "There has been a strange silence," he said. "We have heard almost nothing from them, not even any expression of remorse. I would concur with those who say that these deaths are the result of criminal neglect. Any time there is a needless loss of life, it is a crime."

One unanswered question is whether Imperial Food Products will reopen the plant, which provides more than 200 jobs. Currently the plant is closed and the workers are struggling to make ends meet on unemployment benefits, workmen's compensation, and other meager benefits. Loss of those jobs, even though they pay only four-fifty to six dollars per hour, would be a heavy blow to the town, Miller said.

He also criticized national leaders, President Bush included, for their silence. Of the nation's prominent leaders, only Jackson journeyed here. In a speech to the surviving workers at the Imperial Food plant, he urged them to "turn tragedy into triumph" by unionizing themselves to press their demands for a safe workplace. "Our national leaders should make their presence felt here," the Reverend Miller added. "This is not just a local catastrophe. This was a national catastrophe."

Hamlet was flooded with media in the hours after the disaster. Furthermore, from across the country came donations to help families. Representative William Ford (D-Mo.) arranged for two survivors, Loretta Goodwin and Bobby Quick, a relative by marriage to Mary Quick, to testify in a congressional hearing in support of HR-3160, a bill that would require worker-management health and safety committees in every workplace. "We welcomed the national attention," Reverend Miller said. "If anything positive or redemptive is to come out of this it has to be setting the wheels in motion to make sure something like this never happens again."

Yet during Reverend Jackson's closing meeting with the grieving families, "you could see the collective hurt," Reverend Miller said. "These people were trying to pick up the pieces. What do we do now? Once the organizations have left, the media attention has waned; this community and these people will still be here."

The September 3 fire is not the first assault Hamlet has faced. A sign posted half a block from City Hall declares, "KEEP HAMLET AN 'ALL AMERICAN CITY' . . . KEEP RADIOACTIVE DUMP OUT OF RICHMOND COUNTY!"

Governor Jim Martin has signed an agreement with eight other governors for the construction of the Southeast nuclear waste dump either in Richmond County or on the border between Wake and Chatham Counties, depending on the outcome of ground-core sampling. ChemNuclear, a subsidiary of Waste Management, Inc., a major contributor in 1988 to the Bush-Quayle campaign and to Senator Jesse Helms (R-NC), will be the main user of the dump that would be located on farmland three miles outside Hamlet. One parcel is owned by Amos McManus, a deacon of Reverend Miller's congregation. "He and other members of this community have gone to court to try to block it," Reverend Miller said. "This is a county with a very low median income, with many working poor. It just seems that something is terribly wrong that they would find Richmond County an ideal location for a nuclear waste site. There is a real feeling of bitterness about that."

Under the shade trees outside the Victim Assistance Center, Wanda Lytch and Mary Brown sat grieving. Together, they held a memorial program with a photo of their fellow worker, Jeffery Antonio Webb, twenty-two, who died while rescuing workers from the raging inferno. "I think a lot about Jeff," Lytch said. "He was so full of life. The owners never should have kept those doors locked. They should get the punishment they deserve."

Carolina Crowd Roars at Governor: "Wrong! Wrong! Wrong!!"

People's World

July 2, 2013

RALEIGH, NORTH CAROLINA—Nearly 5,000 protesters at a "Moral Monday" rally here, July 1, roared disapproval of North Carolina Governor Pat McCrory's decision to terminate federal jobless benefits for 70,000 unemployed workers in the Tarheel State that same morning.

The Reverend William Barber, president of the North Carolina NAACP, main sponsor of the protests, accused McCrory of a "bald-faced lie" in claiming that accepting federal funds to extend unemployment compensation would cost the state.

"Zero is the amount of dollars it would have cost this state," Barber thundered. "Seventy thousand unemployed workers lost their benefits at 12:01 this morning. Now they have to worry how they are going to pay for their medicine, pay for food, pay the rent."

An additional 100,000 jobless workers in the state will lose their unemployment benefits in the coming months even though North Carolina ranks fifth in the nation in unemployment, he said.

Added Barber, "The hurt you are doing to unemployed people is wrong. The hurt you are doing to voters is wrong!" The crowd roared back, "Wrong! Wrong! Wrong!"

The rooftop porch of the nearby General Assembly building was packed with legislators and their aides listening to the rally speakers on a day of intermittent rain and flash-flood warnings. As the rally began, the sun burst through.

Barber also blasted McCrory for rejecting Medicaid funding under Obamacare, stripping 500,000 low-income people in North Carolina of their only health coverage.

Barber recalled that Republican leaders described the Voting Rights Act as a "headache" even as they pushed through voter ID requirements that civil rights advocates term "a poll tax by another name."

Barber listed the martyrs who died to win the right to vote, from Medgar Evers to the Reverend Martin Luther King, Jr. "Too much blood has been lost, too many tears," he said. "If you think you have a headache now, just try to take away our voting rights. We're going to fight them because they are wrong. We're going to register everybody, get them to the polls like never before."

The crowd chanted, "Not one step back."

Rabbi Judy Schindler of Temple Beth El in Charlotte reminded the crowd that 600,000 poor children in North Carolina will be hurt by the cutbacks. She hailed the movement of many religious faiths, of all races and genders that is fighting back.

Javan Richardson, a ninth grader from Rocky Mount, recited lines from the Gospel according to Matthew: "For I was hungry and you gave me nothing to eat, I was thirsty and you gave me nothing to drink, I was a stranger and you did not invite me in . . ." The crowd cheered.

Yara Allen, a leader of the Rocky Mount NAACP, pointed at the General Assembly building. "If there is no justice in our house, there should be no peace in that house over there," she said. "We will take this to the polls in the next election."

Later, Allen told the *People's World,* "I've been coming to these rallies since they began and it has just grown bigger each week. We've been out in the rain, when tornadoes were forecast. Today they predicted flash floods. Nothing will stop us. We're here to stay."

She added, "We have become a family over the weeks. We are united across party lines, racial lines, religious lines. We are not going to be diverted by their divide-and-conquer tactics."

There were union members in their caps and jackets with placards upholding union organizing rights—Communications Workers of America (CWA), Service Employees (SEIU), Electrical Workers (UE). Many physicians, who wore their white hospital smocks with stethoscopes around their necks, denounced cutbacks in Medicaid. Teachers in the crowd held signs protesting the drive to privatize public schools in the state. And many in the crowd were campaigning against "fracking" and demanding safe energy and clean air and water.

Harvey Smith told the *People's World* he has been unable to find steady work since he moved to North Carolina twenty-three years ago. He and his wife survive on his unemployment compensation. "After that runs out, I'll have to take early retirement and live on Social Security," he said.

The governor also cut the maximum of those still receiving benefits from $535 per week to $350 a week. He slashed the amount workers are allowed to earn on part-time jobs from $156 per week to $70 per week. He reduced the duration of benefits from twenty-six weeks to as little as twelve weeks.

Smith pointed out that North Carolina's budget director is the notorious Art Pope, owner of hundreds of variety stores in the region, a billionaire who also serves on the board of directors of Koch Industries. McCrory and Pope inflict maximum suffering on the poor while showering giveaways on their wealthy cronies, Smith charged.

Duke University historian Dr. Timothy Tyson scorned Republicans who think the people's movement is a "sinking ship." Said Tyson, "They are wrong. The ship that is sinking is the creaky old ship of white supremacy." The new ship of multiracial unity "is bound for glory. Get on board," he said. "There's room for many a more."

Chapter 3

Disasters—Natural and Man-Made

Disasters have been a rich source of stories for me in my half century as a reporter. Even if the culprit is Mother Nature, I have observed that politicians rush in to claim their share of the blame.

Take President George W. Bush. On his way back from cutting brush on his Texas ranch, Bush ordered Air Force One to circle over New Orleans so he could look out the window at hundreds of residents reeling from Hurricane Katrina, starving on the rooftops of their flood-ravaged homes.

Bush must have imagined that the people below his wing would appreciate his fly by, but Bush got what he deserved: Outrage. He gazed like an emperor at his subjects suffering below, a level of arrogance that flowed naturally from a man who steals votes, who was installed in the White House by a Supreme Court, a very American coup d'état.

Some disaster stories have fallen into my lap like ripe plums. The Teton Dam Break is an example. I was on vacation in the summer of 1976. We were driving west and had just crossed the Grand Tetons into Idaho. Joyce was at the wheel. I was dozing; not performing my co-pilot duties.

We came to a fork in the road and Joyce turned north instead of south to the Interstate. I fumed silently at this navigational error that would cost us an extra day. Here we were, sidetracked onto a narrow two-lane road headed toward Tetonia and Rexburg.

Suddenly, directly ahead of us, smack dab in the middle of the road was a handsome, white-frame farmhouse. What in the devil? About 100-yards to the east was the foundation of the house. Traffic was backed up and slowed to a crawl.

We inched up until we reached an Idaho State Trooper directing traffic. Joyce rolled down the window. "What happened? How did the house get here?" she asked the officer.

"Yesterday, a dam broke a couple of miles east of here and a wall of water floated the house over and dropped it here."

We looked around. In every direction, we saw the devastation. Trees uprooted. Barns smashed to kindling. Houses smashed or floated off their foundations and dropped a hundred, even two-hundred yards downstream.

At that moment, I came off vacation. Thank you, Joyce, for delivering this hot story to me! You can make navigational errors like that anytime.

I wrote up my story and sent it to the *Daily World*.

There were other disaster stories I wrote that I include in this book: Hurricane Charlie stories I wrote from Florida; my trip with Sam Webb, then Chairman of the Communist Party USA, to New Orleans five days after Katrina hit; my return to New Orleans two years later; the near nuclear meltdown at Three Mile Island, Pennsylvania; and the tragic explosion of the space shuttle Challenger in which the entire crew and New Hampshire school teacher, Christa McAullife died.

Even if the "power elite" was not at fault in causing these disasters, they were responsible for reacting to the emergency, for providing assistance to the victims suffering the loss of all the essentials of life. In all the stories I've covered, they failed.

Yet there are also heroes in these stories, people who rushed in to save lives, restore shelter, provide water, food, medical care, electricity. I wrote articles about the Red Cross headquarters in both Fort Meyers, Florida, and Baton Rouge, Louisiana, where teams of emergency workers and armies of volunteers had come to the rescue of hurricane and flood victims. Organized labor was always a factor in these mobilizations.

Yet I still hear ringing in my ears, George W. Bush's smug comment, "Brownie, you're doing a heckuva job." As he congratulated FEMA Director Michael Brown, the people of New Orleans were dying of hunger and thirst, still marooned on their rooftops, still waiting for FEMA to bring water and food.

The earthen dam on the Teton River in Idaho breaks. Photo courtesy of U.S. Departmenbt of the Interior, Bureau of Reclamation.

Teton Dam Break: A Not So Natural Disaster
World Magazine

August 7, 1976
SUGAR CITY, IDAHO—The waters of the Teton River rise in the snowy Teton Mountains directly east of here and flow westward across the wide plain of eastern Idaho. The river supplies the water for a vast irrigation system that has transformed the sere brown desert into a lush emerald green garden—sugar beets, potatoes, alfalfa, and corn. But at 11:57 a.m. on June 5th, the river

delivered the people of this valley a near fatal blow. The Teton earth dam broke, sending a wall of water fifteen feet high raging across the farmland.

Two crawler tractor drivers, Owen Daley and Jack McGraw, worked frantically bulldozing rocks and gravel into the breach in the dam right up to the final moment. Finally, their giant machines slipped downward towards the swirling maelstrom. They leaped to safety at the last instant. The dam gave way, releasing 130,000 acre feet of water in one ferocious rush.

Six weeks later, the valley looks like a scene of brutal warfare. Handsome frame farmhouses lie smashed like kindling. Many were ripped from their foundations and shoved 100 feet or more by the onrushing water and deposited broken and warped in the middle of fields.

We drove through the area on our way to Oregon for a vacation. Two days earlier, we had passed through Rapid City, South Dakota, which is still suffering the after effects of the devastating flood of June 9, 1972, when a dam broke, drowning 300 and destroying a large part of the town.

In the Teton dam break, eleven people died. The postmaster in Tetonia told us the exact number is disputed because while three died as direct victims of the water, eight more have died since from heart attacks or shock when they viewed the total destruction to their land and homes. The statistics of the disaster are appalling: more than $1 billion in losses including 773 homes destroyed, 13,725 head of livestock killed, 99,252 acres of land ruined, 3,571 farm buildings demolished. The dam itself cost $55 million and the loss of irrigation potential from the dam break is incalculable.

Since June 5, more than 3,000 people have applied for unemployment compensation.

We drove along the ruins of Highway 33 for more than twenty miles through Newdale, Sugar City, and Rexburg, all a scene of total annihilation. A white frame house with a handsome veranda had been set down squarely in the middle of the highway just outside Rexburg, and dump trucks, earth moving equipment and cars now detour through a ruined potato field to get around it. The bathtub that once went with the house lay two hundred feet away, mired in mud. Farm implements dotted the landscape, twisted, rusting hulks. A brand new John Deere tractor had been rolled over and over by the flood and lay upside down, buried in mud, its wheels in the air like the carcass of some bizarre prehistoric dinosaur.

Sugar City, once a quiet tree shaded town that served the farmers of this area is a ghost town. Not a single house was spared and every family has been evacuated. The cottonwoods have been uprooted and on Main Street the windows are smashed and the doors stand ajar.

In the next town, Rexburg, the people are struggling to clean up the wreckage, shoveling mud from the modern elementary school, the houses, and businesses, repairing streets, water, sewage and electricity. But the pace of the recovery appeared painfully slow and the people we talked to seemed dazed by the disaster. They labored all their lives to build up this land, and lived in beautiful white farmhouses. Now they are waiting for delivery of mobile homes that will be their only shelter for years— some say permanently.

Anger is in their voices when they speak of the duplicity of the Federal officials who designed and operated the dam. They are suspicious that the government will withhold the level of assistance necessary to restore the valley.

"I lost everything," said Earl Dayton, owner of a tiny service station in Tetonia. "My place is across the river. There wasn't a fence post left standing. It tore out all my apple trees, my pines. I'm living in a mobile home now. It isn't hooked up yet but I slept there last night anyway."

The builder of the dam was the Morrison-Knudsen Company of Boise, a giant building contractor that won notoriety for its profiteering as Pentagon contractor in Vietnam during the Indochina war. Their construction methods stirred suspicions when a woman geologist analyzed the clay earth they were using as fill and reported to the Federal Bureau of Reclamation that it was unsuitable because it percolates water at a danger-ously rapid rate. Her warnings were ignored and this pattern of cover-up continued right up to the moment of the disaster. "An hour before the dam broke they were still saying 'There's nothing to worry about'," Earl Dayton said. "People who lived near the dam called the Bureau of Reclamation because they knew the water level was so high. There was no advance warning at all."

The bitter experience of victims of past disasters is known here in June, 1972, the victims of Hurricane Agnes in Wilkes Barre, Pennsylvania, lost their homes when the Susquehanna River flooded. President Nixon flew over the Wilkes Barre disaster in a helicopter—but all the sympathy was for Bethlehem Steel which suffered damage to its mill. The people were forced into mobile homes which the Federal government promised would be "temporary." They are living there still. A similar fate was suffered by the victims of Hurricane Camille in the Gulf States and by the victims of the Rapid City, South Dakota dam break. They are examples of the govern-ment's indifference to the people while lavishing billions of tax dollars on the Pentagon and big business.

Glen C. Scott, owner of a custom meat packing plant, who is also a Jefferson County Commissioner, referred to these past experiences and predicted a fight to win the assistance necessary to restore the valley.

"There's a lot of feeling here that the same thing will happen here as happened in other places," he said. "After all the hoopla and excitement has died down, the disaster will be forgotten and we will be left with our mobile homes," he said.

Scott, who lost his home and suffered severe damage to his business, had high praise for the thousands of volunteers from throughout Idaho and Utah who rushed to assist the flood victims.

"There are still a lot of good people left in this world," he said, "We had help coming from hundreds of miles away. They came and worked for nothing for hours. Many worked fourteen hour days helping us to clean up."

The hardest blow of all, though, was to the farmland itself. The economic lifeblood of the area is this rich land and today one drives for miles through land that has been stripped of its topsoil, clawed with deep ravines that gash the once flat terrain.

"Madison County was just annihilated," 'said Scott. "The damage to the farmlands [will] probably never get repaired."

Cathy Surrey, a young woman clerk at the Idaho Drugstore in Rigby spoke emotionally of the destruction to neighboring Rexburg. "It's not a very big place, you know. They were just getting started with the college there and now it's all been wiped out. I don't know if it will ever be the same. All my aunts and uncles lost everything they had."

Three Mile Island: Nuclear Cloud Travels 20 Miles
Daily World

May 30, 1979
MIDDLETOWN, PENNSYLVANIA, MARCH 29—The Geiger counters of the U.S. Nuclear Regulatory Commission (NRC) crackled here today as a radioactive breeze blew across the Susquehanna River from a leaking nuclear reactor owned by Metropolitan Edison Company.

The radiation leaked through four feet of concrete from the electric power station's No. 2 reactor yesterday spreading an irradiated cloud twenty miles up-river past Harrisburg and down-river towards Wilkes Barre.

Phillip Stohr, an NRC observer, holding a Geiger counter, was on duty this morning at a mobile lab parked across the river from Three Mile Island, where the giant station is located. The radiation level on the meter, .1 milliroentgen per hour, is five times the normal level, he said.

Edison officials claimed today the leak was caused by the shutdown of cooling system pumps, causing the nuclear core to overheat. Unknown numbers of the 36,000 uranium fuel rods ruptured. The buildup of super-heated steam inside the reactor was so intense that the company ordered contaminated vapor vented to the atmosphere to prevent an explosion.

Not cooling down

Edison Case, deputy director of the NRC, told reporters, "The reactor core is not cooling down as fast as we would like."

Case said more than 60,000 gallons of water have been flooded into the reactor room, which was still 550 degrees after being shut down.

Construction workers at the plant were going across the bridge today and into the reactor room despite radiation levels that are 1,000 times above normal. The company acknowledged the extreme danger of radiation poisoning to these workers by limiting the crews to a one-hour shift in the reactor room.

Donald John, a nuclear welder preparing to don his anti-radiation protective gear and respirator to go into the plant, told me, "We are going in for an hour and then we'll come out. Our job is going to be to pin the main stream hangars in the reactor."

The workers are represented by Local 250 of the Plumbers and Pipefitters in Harrisburg, which, John said, is monitoring the accident, the worst ever to occur in a nuclear power station.

Insufficient knowledge

"I've worked here ten years," he said. "I've got a wife and three kids. We live in Middletown. I'm not opposed to nuclear power, but they don't know enough about these low levels of exposure to radiation."

David Littleton, another nuclear welder on his way to the reactor room, said, "I've worked for one year under radioactive conditions. The company sets the limitations on our exposure. It's up to the Nuclear Regulatory Commission to come up with a decision on what really happened here. I definitely want a full investigation."

George W. Boyer, owner of Bucklock Market, a tiny grocery store in the shadow of the power station's mammoth cooling towers, said the company had not even bothered to inform residents of the leak.

Workers mop up radioactive waters from the leaking containment at Three Mile Island, Photo courtesy of Nuclear Regulatory Agency.

"I didn't even know about it until a neighbor came in and said there was an accident," Boyer said. "I didn't know whether he meant a strike or what. Then we heard on the news of a 'slight leak.' The company is very secretive about it. As far as big companies are concerned, I don't trust any of them. They lie. They cover up as much as possible."

Unsafe materials

Workers at the station who buy at his market, Boyer continued, "told me they have had a lot of difficulties on No. 2 reactor. I'm an old pipefitter myself. I was interested in the stainless steel pipe they use. It's beautiful stuff. But does it have enough strength?"

Immediately after the accident, Boyer said, Edison Company wanted to reactivate No. 1 reactor, which has been shut down since February for refueling. "But the NRC wouldn't let them," he said. "The company didn't want to lose any money. It's a big corporation. They are all the same."

The setting for this accident was idyllic: A perfect spring day with the Susquehanna flowing majestically through the rolling Pennsylvania Dutch farm country. But up-river at Steeltown, Pennsylvania, thousands of Bethlehem Steel workers and their families, exposed daily to fumes from Bethlehem's coke batteries, now have another worry; exposure to Edison Company's nuclear radiation.

John Wagenknecht, on his way to classes at a nearby community college, paused to comment on the accident. "It's really terrible," he said, "Who knows how many abnormal babies might result from this kind of carelessness? And the company didn't even inform the state authorities about the accident until it had been leaking for four hours."

Challenger Disaster Linked to Reagan Star Wars
Daily World

February 20, 1986
WASHINGTON----The death of the seven Challenger astronauts has cast a glaring light on the fatal consequences of President Reagan's drive for corporate deregulation and budget cuts.

Challenger Shuttle explodes during liftoff. Photo courtesy of NASA.

NASA reports on previous mishaps now ring with foreboding of disaster that were obviously ignored by an administration hell-bent on profits and military supremacy in space.

On March 5, 1985, a platform at the Orbiter Processing Facility (OPF) at Kennedy Space Center collapsed seriously injuring a worker and inflicting $200,000 damage to one of the shuttle's payload bay doors.

NASA's report declared, "This mishap can be characterized as the logistical culmination of a series of events and conditions which pushed the mechanical components beyond their limits."

The report cited Lockheed Services, the subcontractor, for "improper operation, improper instruction in operating procedures, violation of NASA and OSHA safety rules, wide use of incidental operators, poor tagout-lockout procedures, incompatibilities between design and operational use and inadequate maintenance. Lockheed was responsible for the operation and maintenance of the Orbiter Payload Bay Access Platform at the time of the mishap."

The report describes in shocking detail the deteriorated condition of critical elements in cranes, winches, cable, chains and other machinery used to lift satellites and other cargo into the shuttle bay.

"After the mishap," the report states, "inspection of the linkage assemblies in all eight of the Platforms showed that most of the master links were elongated, indicating that they had been overstressed at some time."

The report adds: "If the regular inspections required by OSHA (Occupational Safety and Health Administration) had been performed, the inevitable discovery of the elongated links would probably have precipitated an investigation. This could have prevented the mishap of March 8."

Reagan, his former secretary of labor, Raymond Donovan and OSHA administrator Thorne Auchter have waged a vendetta against the health and safety agency, slashing OSHA's budget and sharply reducing the number of on-site inspections and inspectors.

The NASA report points out that personnel to operate the cranes are required, by regulation, to "be expert in the operation and maintenance of this equipment. However, most of the several hundred personnel who are certified to operate the platform, do so only incidentally to their primary duties."

This is a perfect example of the drive by big business in their factories, mines and mills to save money by eliminating the job classification system so employers can freely shift workers from one task to another, even if it means they are unfamiliar with the dangerous equipment they are operating. The report blames the practice at the launch sites on the "schedule-driven environment."

NASA last Friday released a compilation of documents it has presented to the Presidential Commission on the January 28 explosion of the Challenger. Included is a Space Transportation System (STS) Change Request filed by J.B. Jackson on December 17, 1982, over three years before the Challenger disaster, warning that the 'O' rings that seal the joints in the casing of the solid rocket booster could fail. Failure of the rings, he wrote, would mean "loss of mission, vehicle, and crew due to metal erosion, burnthrough, and probable case burst resulting in fire and deflagration."

Indeed, NASA engineers now concede that may have been the cause of the Challenger explosion. Yet Jackson's request for action was rejected.

Katrina: Clean-Up Begins, Anger Won't Wash Away
From: *RedNet, People's Weekly World Newspaper*
By *Tim Wheeler*

September 15, 2005
NEW ORLEANS—Two weeks after Hurricane Katrina devastated this region, and as they begin a valiant struggle to rebuild, people here are still fuming that the Bush administration was so tardy in coming to their aid.

"I heard my mayor begging for help," said Robert Mitchell as he and his fellow crewmembers raked debris on Royal Street in the French Quarter. "Yet three days after this Category Five hurricane hit, where was the help? There was no help."

Mitchell was toiling in the hot sun amid reeking mounds of garbage. He lives on the West Bank, a part of New Orleans mostly spared from the floodwaters but damaged by the winds. "The head of FEMA knew this storm was coming, but he was on vacation. The hurricane couldn't be avoided. But the death and misery afterward could have been avoided. There was no relief."

In a four-day tour of the hurricane zone from Houston to Baton Rouge and on to New Orleans this reporter and traveling companion Sam Webb, chairman of the Communist Party USA, did not hear a kind word for the leadership of FEMA or any other top Bush administration official.

"When the Saints Come Marching In" watercolor sketch by author of Jackson Square, New Orleans, Thanksgiving, 2007

Webb said, "The harrowing stories that people told brought home so hard the irresponsibility and criminality of the Bush administration. To make people's lives livable, it will take the full commitment of the federal government and a people's watchdog committee."

The scope of the catastrophe is enormous: an estimated one million people homeless, 90,000 square miles of the Gulf Coast in ruins, 293,000 houses destroyed or damaged, and a death toll of more than 600 that is rising daily.

The U.S. Forestry Service opened a field kitchen in the French Quarter where we stopped for breakfast the morning of September 12. It was crowded with National Guard and 82nd Airborne troops, firefighters, medics and utility workers from across the nation. Paratroopers are going door to door in still-flooded neighborhoods, searching for the dead. On September 11, they finally reached Memorial Hospital and recovered at least forty-five bodies. Earlier, rescue crews found an additional thirty-four bodies in the Saint Rita Nursing Home.

One EMS medic from Ashtabula County, Ohio, gave us hepatitis and tetanus shots, reflecting the grave danger of disease from the foul slime engulfing the city. "Bush says the head of FEMA did a `heck of a job,'" he said. "Five of the top eight positions in FEMA are held by people who are unqualified. That's criminal!" he told the *World*. "There has been a massive misallocation of resources here."

Sitting nearby was Javier Rosado, one of a handful of people who refused to evacuate. "I've got bottled water, canned food and a portable generator. I'm a survivor."

"I'm from Puerto Rico," he said. "Once we had three hurricanes in seven days. FEMA could have saved a lot of lives if they had sent in the military earlier. When Ivan struck Florida last year, the military was there, FEMA came in handing out money. But here eighty percent of the population is Black." Indeed, FEMA halted a program of handing out debit cards with $2,000 in cash, forcing the victims to fill out pages of paperwork to apply for financial aid.

The grim discovery at Memorial Hospital overshadowed President George W. Bush's New Orleans September 12 visit. Bush was staying on the Iwo Jima, an airborne assault carrier moored just down river. "Bush's role in this really sucks," Rosado said. "I regret to say I voted for him."

On his return to the White House, Bush held an East Room press conference and admitted "personal responsibility" for the botched federal response. He also accepted the resignation of FEMA Director Michael Brown.

Gwen Knight, a volunteer from San Diego, was on duty at the field kitchen serving paper plates heaped with scrambled eggs, ham and hash browns. She gestured to the empty, silent restaurants on Decatur Street. "They're usually full of people," she said. "Now it's like a ghost town and we're the only restaurant open in New Orleans. I dropped everything and volunteered to come here. We're going to be here thirty days, and longer if we are needed. We did the same during a big wildfire in Nevada, feeding all the forest firefighters."

In Jackson Square, a crew of twenty Navajo forest firefighters from Fort Defiance, Ariz., was cutting up downed oaks and magnolias with chain saws. "This is a really historic part of New Orleans," said the crew leader, Marvin Sanderson.

"We are trying to preserve as many as possible of the trees that are still alive. The last disaster we worked was the forest fire in the Cave Creek complex in North Phoenix."

Fashionable Canal Street with its Saks Fifth Avenue, Shell Oil tower, Hyatt Regency, Hilton and other luxury hotels was a scene of devastation, the streets littered with broken glass, downed power lines and an ooze that coated the pavement. But reconstruction is already in high gear.

The streets were clogged with police cruisers, National Guard Humvees and cherry-picker utility trucks that have poured in from across the nation.

The Bush administration has already doled out a $100 million reconstruction contract to the Shaw Group, a wealthy construction firm. Shaw is handing out flyers at shelters asking engineers, electricians and other skilled workers to apply for jobs. Next in line are Bechtel, Fluor and Halliburton, all with close crony ties to the Bush administration. The administration has announced it will nullify the Davis-Bacon Prevailing Wage Act in the Gulf region to insure even heftier profits for these giant construction firms.

From the elevated expressway that loops around the West Bank, we observed an eerie spectacle: miles of working-class and poor neighborhoods without a human being in sight, nothing moving, no traffic, some of them still flooded. We drove past miles of wrecked stores, shopping malls and service stations, all empty. What will be done to rebuild these neighborhoods so the people can return?

Thomas Garner, a lifelong New Orleans resident and an employee of an insurance company, had at least part of an answer. He was sitting in front of a television with scores of other evacuees at the Red Cross Shelter in Baton Rouge.

The underdog New Orleans Saints had just defeated the Carolina Panthers on a field goal in the last seven seconds. "After all we've been through, it was an inspiration that they won," he said. "The city is coming back stronger than ever. The federal government has known about the weakness of the levees for forty years. All our legislators and congresspersons have been predicting this disaster. But the federal government chose to spend the money somewhere else."

The federal government has appropriated $62 billion for relief. "It's a major concern that too much of that money is not being allocated for the purpose of rebuilding but rather to line somebody's pockets," Garner said. "We need to allocate that money to the people who need it."

He assailed Bush's decision to nullify the Davis-Bacon wage law. "Give workers jobs rebuilding this region. Pay them the wages they are entitled to," he said. "They will spend that money and it will help rebuild the city."

Making Dry Bones Come Alive in New Orleans
By Tim Wheeler

October 12, 2007
NEW ORLEANS—It takes a leap of faith to believe that this lovely city can be rebuilt from the devastation of Hurricane Katrina, given the cruelty of President Bush who concealed his administration's abandonment of the working people of New Orleans with honey-sweet promises, all of them broken.

Yet on the marquee outside the gutted Mt. Carmel Missionary Ministries church in the Lower 9th Ward is posted this message from the Holy Scriptures: "Can these bones live? O, ye dry bones, hear the word of the Lord. . . . These bones shall live!"

The church is the only building still standing for blocks in any direction after the levee broke August 29, 2005, unleashing a twenty-five-foot wall of water that smashed everything in its path.

What the water didn't destroy, bulldozers have leveled in the two years since, leaving acre after acre of empty, weed-infested lots where houses once stood.

Further away from the levees, thousands more houses that could be repaired stand vacant while the owners struggle against stalling tactics on the delivery of "Road Home" grants to rebuild.

'I grew up here'

As I was pondering that passage from the Prophet Ezekiel, Randy Gibson drove up and got out of his car. He is one of many thousands forced to flee Katrina who has now returned, helping push the city's population back up to sixty percent of its pre-Katrina population.

"I grew up here. My whole life was here," Gibson told the *World*. "I moved away the day before the hurricane hit. My wife and I ended up in Lakeworth, Florida. I worked as a mailman. Now I'm back working as a letter carrier here in New Orleans. We're so shorthanded, I work until nine or ten o'clock every night, so I don't get back down here as often as I'd like."

He pointed toward the levees along the Industrial Canal to the west. "My house was right over there on Tennessee Street," he said. "It's gone. The barge that broke through the levee that night was sitting right there. It was bigger than this church."

Then he spoke wistfully of the past. "New Orleans is a party town and nowhere more so than in the Lower 9th Ward," he said, right around the corner from the church was a nightclub.

"We'd spend Saturday nights there listening to jazz," he said. "When we came out at dawn, the congregation of this church was already arriving for Sunday morning services." Underlining the vibrancy off that culture is the nearby home of Fats Domino, still standing defiantly in the Lower 9th Ward with the initial's "FD" on its bright yellow facade.

Gibson added, "To come here now and see all this devastation, it's unreal. It's unbelievable. This was a disaster in America. What is the problem with coming in here and rebuilding this whole community?

"You talk about billions," he continued. "Congress just approved another $50 billion for Iraq. Why can't the federal government just print up that money and use it to rebuild here? If this neighborhood was up and running, there would be parties on every block for every Saints game."

Fighting greedy developers

A few blocks nearer the levee is the "Blue House," headquarters of the Common Ground Relief Center that played a heroic role in the days immediately after Katrina. Common Ground, with the help of Veterans for Peace, opened the first emergency medical center after the flood. It was staffed by doctors, nurses and other health care professionals at a time when the city's hospitals were flooded and abandoned.

Common Ground and its tireless leader, Malik Rahim, orchestrated much of the volunteer efforts in the two years since to "muck" people's houses and help them begin to rebuild. An estimated 1.1 million people have worked as volunteers in New Orleans since Katrina. It might be the greatest, most sustained volunteer effort ever.

Yet the crisis in the Lower 9th is unabated, fueled by the greed of developers who see Katrina as a golden opportunity for wholesale "urban removal" of 127,000 people—mostly poor African Americans. Volunteer Calvin Bernard was on duty at Blue House. Common Ground, together with ACORN, now has shifted their focus to stopping the developers from wholesale theft of property of families displaced from the Lower 9th Ward. Bernard, a construction worker, was working on a job site in Baton Rouge when the levees broke. His home, with his wife trapped inside, was swept away. Her body was found eight months later.

Now Bernard works every day helping Katrina survivors, or planting lawn signs with the words, "Stop Land Grab" and "Stop the Bulldozers."

Common Ground initiated a project of placing house numbers on the lots where houses once stood to protect the property rights of homeowners forced to flee and who now lack the resources to return and rebuild.

"Three families have come here today planning to begin remodeling their homes," Bernard continued. "They found out the city had bulldozed their houses without informing them in advance. The big land developers want all this land. But they aren't going to get it as long as I'm living."

The New Orleans diaspora

Of the estimated 200,000 who evacuated New Orleans before and after Katrina, only an estimated 31,000 have returned. The other 170,000 are scattered in every state of the union, with heavy concentrations in Baton Rouge, Houston, Dallas, San Antonio, Atlanta, Memphis, and southeast Mississippi.

The Times-Picayune newspaper featured a front-page report on this "diaspora" September 2. While some of the evacuees are building new lives, many more are homesick and drive back long distances to visit the sites of their damaged or destroyed homes, the Times reported. Others are returning because FEMA has terminated hurricane relief benefits and they cannot find jobs, affordable housing or health care in the cities where they took refuge. Many also face the pressure of rising discrimination and racist hostility.

A tale of two cities

My son, Morgan, a union electrician, is working as a volunteer after his regular job. He drove me around the Lower 9th Ward, introducing me to some of the volunteers and residents he has assisted.

Then we headed across town to the Garden District. "This is still a tale of two cities," he said, echoing Charles

Dickens, as we cruised beside Audubon Park, an immaculate green oasis with magnificent 200-year-old oaks and a manicured golf course. Wealthy residents were strolling on the grass or jogging beneath the spreading boughs.

On St. Charles Avenue stood the entrance to Audubon Place, a community protected by tall wrought iron fences and a gatehouse. A sign posted outside warns, "Illegal to enter." Beyond the bars stand the dazzling white mansions of the rich with their fluted columns and sweeping verandas.

The floodwaters never reached this fabulously wealthy enclave, Morgan said. "They may have evacuated, but the houses they returned to were as gleaming as when they left."

Morgan then drove me back to Treme Vieux Carre, the neighborhood where he lives with a crew of electricians from Guatemala working in the rebuilding effort.

Nearby is a big public housing complex, handsome brick buildings surrounded by neatly trimmed lawns. They are now boarded up and posted with menacing signs warning trespassers not to enter. While I was there, former residents, members of the Hurricane Katrina Relief Fund, staged a sit-in at the New Orleans Housing Authority demanding that these apartments be repaired and reopened to help ease the acute shortage of affordable rental housing.

Soon after the floodwaters began to subside in New Orleans, professor Scott Myers-Lipton of San Jose State University in California launched a campaign to push through Congress what he calls the "Gulf Coast Civic Works Project" (GCCWP), a program to employ 100,000 Gulf Coast residents in federally funded jobs rebuilding schools, hospitals, libraries, streets, sidewalks and other infrastructure in cities and towns on the Gulf Coast. The campaign has caught fire, especially on campuses. Now students enlisted in the campaign are attending the debates of the Democratic and Republican presidential contenders to ask them questions like: "If elected president of the U.S., would you introduce legislation based on the Gulf Coast Civic Works Project? Do you support the idea of a WPA-like project to rebuild the Gulf Coast?" One of the links provided on the GCCWP website features more than 100 photographs of the magnificent reconstruction of public buildings in New Orleans during the Great Depression by unemployed workers hired through the Works Progress Administration. It includes restoration of some of New Orleans' architectural treasures in the French Quarter, such as the house where Gen. Andrew Jackson lived during the 1812 Battle of New Orleans, and the St. Roch Public Market, already 100 years old in 1937. Now that market is closed and falling into ruins. All this begs the question: Why not a new WPA program to rebuild New Orleans?

A weeklong visit to the Crescent City brought home an inescapable reality: The devastation here is too immense ever to be rebuilt by volunteers or profit-driven developers. Only the federal government has the resources to rebuild this city. Use the tax dollars we have already turned over to them time and time again, the lion's share now gobbled up in the endless war in Iraq. The program must guarantee a controlling voice for the people of New Orleans, including those displaced across the nation who still hope to take that "road home." The federally funded jobs must include strong affirmative action guarantees and protection of union rights.

If we can make this an overriding issue in the 2008 elections and bring it to reality after the elections, then the "dry bones" of New Orleans will indeed live again.

Burnt Offering in Baltimore
Daily World

In memory of Gerald Burton Gloss—August 1, 1979

August 8, 1979

Singing "Praise the Lord" the deaf preacher
old as Baltimore, proclaims the gospel joy
strewing loaves of week-old Wonder Bread

to outstretched hands. He almost hears
the angry shouts, cries of pain, grief, the
crash of fenders on wrong-way cars up one-way
streets—the human tumult rolling down like
the waters of River Jordan, as tears on a woman's
cheeks. From this trouble, the prophet divines
the mysterious Hand, the Second Coming, sees
heaven close as petals of a pale rose bloom
in Mrs. Stewart's backyard, smells it fragrant
as honeysuckle on summer verandas and strong
as hymns in his youth of rich-voiced Black women.
He is ready to enter paradise, as in
passing through his creaking front yard gate.
Yet in his hope seized from pain at the dying
young is suffering still too deep
for rivers of tears to wash away.

At three a.m., the pumper from Engine
Company Number Nine hurtles down his
sleeping street, blaring prophecies, unfalse
alarms, toward infernos, smoke inhalations,
second-degree burns over sixty percent of
tender child bodies. Kneeling on the caved-in
Porch roof of 523 St. George's Street,
his soot black face lighted garishly by flood lamps
that render life into stage drama, the firefighter
is mouth-to-mouth with Gerald, age eight, and
blowing, blowing, blowing the breath of life
into the lifeless child form—last lingering
life-wishing kiss of farewell. Sweat trickles
like rivers of Jordan down his weeping brow.
From night-gowned women and shivering men below,
waiting like the chorus in a Sophoclean horror
play, a sigh goes up of life expiring.
The child is dead. His mother, still
reaching up the incinerated stairs, lies
dead. His infant sister, dead in her smoking
crib. Such are the burnt offerings of
Slum-dwellers to Molochs of Real

Estate and other Golden calves. There is
no balm to sooth the searing wounds, no
mercy in heaven for these earthly crimes.
Summer storm clouds gather black, splitting
the sky with jagged lightning. White,
hot rains pelt the parched earth. Rage
in human, not godlike form, thunders down
the Jordan River banks

TIM WHEELER

Author interviews residents of NE Washington, D.C. about deadly
house fire. Photo by Ray Pinkson.

Infants Die in Cribs as Congress Cuts Firefighting Funds
Daily World

September 18, 1976
WASHINGTON—As the people of Northeast Washington
grieved, three-year-old Megan Chandler and her one-
year-old brother, Mecca, were buried on September 11.
The two infants burned to death in their cribs the night
of September 8, while a fire-fighting unit three blocks
away was "off-duty" due to Congressional budget cuts.

They were laid to rest in tiny coffins in a cemetery near their fire-gutted row house on tree-lined Neal Street, only eleven blocks from the U.S. Capitol.

The death of the infants, despite the despite the desperate efforts of D.C. firefighters to save them, has convulsed the neighborhood with grief and rage. Yet Engine Company Number 10 remained idle again on September 11, its gleaming pumper trucks unmanned in the station house during the crew's days off.

Firemen laid off

The U.S. Congress, which just approved President Ford's $120 billion Pentagon budget, cut the D.C. firefighter's budget by $1 million, forcing layoff of four relief crews. Four fire stations in the nation's capital are now open only on a rotating shift.

Milton C. Chandler, uncle of the dead children, who shared their home at 1258 Neal Street, fought back tears as he told the *Daily World* of the conflagration that swept his home while he had been away.

"I came back home and found all the fire equipment here and they told me that my niece and nephew were dead. My niece would come running out when I came home from work and she would shout, 'Uncle Milton."

"Everybody on this block loved those kids. The neighbors would take them across the street to play on the playground."

He stared at the sodden, fire-scorched children's clothes, the ruined mattresses, and the remains of furniture piled in the front yard. "My mother is taking it awful hard," he said. "She came over here this morning to see if she could find anything worth saving. She found the china cabinet, but looking at it made her so sick she just left."

Department off duty

"If the Fire Department had been on duty when the fire broke out Mecca and Megan would be alive today."

Mary Hughes, a neighbor up the block, said she would attend the protest meeting that evening at the Martin Luther King Memorial Center, right next door to the Fire House on Florida Ave.

"They've got money to do everything else, but no money to keep the fire stations open," she said, her voice hard with anger. "People are living in fear of their lives. We pay $400 in taxes every year on this raggedy old house and that's supposed to pay for fire protection."

She pointed out that this was not the first fatal fire. Last February a house 580 feet from the station house caught fire and a thirteen-year-old child died. Seven houses on Todd Place burned recently because of the slow response by the fire department.

The people in the neighborhood had high praise for the Black and white firemen who suffered serious injuries trying to save the Chandler children.

No water available

A hook and ladder company, which shares the same fire house with Engine Company Number 10, was the first to arrive at the scene. But without the pumpers of Engine Company Number 10, they were without water to fight the blaze.

Private Phillip Degan placed a ladder at a second story window and attempted to climb through a holocaust of smoke and flame, but was forced back.

Lieutenant Ronald Harman charged through the front door and up the stairway, engulfed in flames and smoke. He was dragged from the inferno by his comrades and rushed to a hospital suffering from burns and smoke inhalation.

A burning wall collapsed on Private Arthur Bykowski when he entered the house to search for the children, and he too was rushed to the hospital.

Finally, after nearly five minutes, the pumper from the nearest fire house arrived—fourteen blocks away. Usual response time is fifty seconds.

Mother in shock

Mecca was found dead in his crib, ten feet from the bedroom window. Beside him was Megan. Patricia Chandler, their mother, barely escaped with her life and has been in shock since.

G.P. Capps, Captain of the hook and ladder company, told the *Daily World* in an interview at the station house, "The only thing that is going to save us is for Congress to restore the money that was taken away."

David Ryan, president of the D.C. Firefighter's Union, said the rotating shift policy is like playing a grisly game of "roulette" with the lives of people. "Today it was two small children in the Northeast. Tomorrow it could be ten people in the Northwest. No one really knows," he said.

This afternoon, the children of Wheatley Elementary School on Neal Street spilled out of the schoolhouse doors as classes ended during this first week of school. The girls wore pigtails and brilliant red, green, blue and purple dresses. The boys chased each other, shouting noisily as they came down the street towards the charred remains of the Chandler house. The two fire-blackened, paneless windows, stared down at the children as they passed by.

144 Beaumont Avenue

When Children Die
People's Daily World

August 20, 1986
BALTIMORE—The young mother, tears flowing, screamed into the night. "My baby! My baby! Let me go!" Several neighbors and three police officers struggled to restrain her from racing into a burning house to rescue her trapped child.

For more than two hours last Thursday evening, the flames leaped from every window in the big three-story wooden frame dwelling at 544 Beaumont Avenue where two children were trapped.

Dickie Davis arrived just past midnight, before the fire engines. Asleep in his house half a block away, he heard screams. He pulled on his jeans, dashed from the house and up the block to the fire. He found his neighbor holding her child, Antoine Jeffery Hoke. "I can't get him to wake up," she cried, shaking the child.

Davis laid the four-year-old on the hood of a car and began mouth to mouth resuscitation. "I brought him around once and then he stopped breathing again," Davis told this reporter. "I worked on him some more, pumping his stomach to force the smoke from his lungs, blowing into his mouth. He started breathing for a few seconds, and I lost him again. Then an ambulance came. I picked Jeffery up, carried him over. They put him on the oxygen mask."

Davis' quick action saved the child, who is now in serious condition at University Hospital. Also treated for burns and smoke inhalation were Caesar Prince, forty-five, and Shirley Hill, fifty.

At 3:45 a.m., when the fire was finally under control, firemen entered the house. They found the body of Deshawn Harper, nine, lying on the stairwell between the second and third floor. On the third floor, lying below a window, was Tiandra Harris, five. In a basement apartment was the body of sixty-eight-year-old Albert Barnes. A victim of emphysema, Barnes breathed with the assistance of an oxygen cylinder.

Fire inspectors believe the blaze started with faulty wiring in the ceiling of Barnes' single room apartment. When the flames reached his oxygen cylinder, it exploded, blowing through the first floor and turning the entire house into a holocaust. Designed as a single family dwelling, the house was divided into twenty rooms. "It's like a barracks in there," declared firefighter Richard Lowman. "There are bedrooms everywhere."

At the time of the fire, fifteen people lived in the house. Used as a shelter for the homeless, the Baltimore Department of Social Services housed as many as twenty-three persons there at one time.

Andre West, who lives three houses down on Beaumont Avenue, said that Mrs. Gladys Harris, resident owner of the house, "took in people sent to her by DSS, welfare recipients, homeless people. They took in babies with nowhere to turn."

Twice before—in 1973 and in 1979—the house burned, West said. In the first blaze, two girls died. In the second another girl died. "They rebuilt this place inside and out," West said. "Now it has burned a third time. In those three fires, six people have died."

Residents say Mayor William Donald Schaefer should be called to account. Last year the firehouse nearest 544 Beaumont was closed in a service cutback. It took the engines seven minutes to arrive at the scene. Community leaders are also condemning his practice of "warehousing" the poor in firetraps like 544 Beaumont Avenue. A plague of house fires in Baltimore during his twelve years in office has claimed the lives of scores of people. In one fire two years ago, eight family members, including five children, died when a candle ignited a curtain. The family was lighting their home with candles because Baltimore Gas & Electric had turned off the power.

Derek Propalis, president of the Winston-Govans Neighborhood Improvement Association, said, "The question you have to ask is what is the nature of the economic beast that requires twenty-three people to live in a house designed for six or seven? When it comes to descent, affordable housing . . . obviously, not enough has been done. We have 40,000 people on waiting lists for public housing in Baltimore. We have a need for 100,000 units of low cost housing just to meet the need."

Fire-gutted houses, boarded and abandoned, are among Baltimore's most widespread landmarks notwithstanding Mayor Schaefer's "Baltimore is Best" hype. The thousands burned from their homes doubled up with neighbors and relatives in the remaining firetraps.

Today, Ivory Harris, grandfather of Deshawn Harper and Tiandra Harris, sat on the porch of neighbors who have taken him in. "I've lost three of my five grandchildren in the past year—two of them in the fire," he said, gazing dejectedly down the street towards the charred ruins of his home. "It's tough. There's nothing we can do but take them to the burial ground."

Financial contributions and donations of clothing for the survivors can be sent to the home of Mrs. Cedril West, 538 Beaumont Avenue, Baltimore, Maryland 21212.

Postscript: The house destroyed in this story is three blocks west of our house on Beaumont Ave. in the Govans neighborhood of Baltimore. Our house has now been destroyed in an arson fire, one of 12 homes in our community destroyed by a deranged arsonist in the past decade. Luckily, no one died. Our granddaughter, Erin, set up a "GoFundMe" website and friends and neighbors contributed over $17,000 to her father and his family who barely escaped but lost everything else. The vast majority of humanity are decent, caring people.

Chapter 4

An Innocent Abroad

My interpreter, Damba, and Mongolian school children chat with me about the "land of Caravans" during my visit in December, 1967.

A Visit To The Land Of Caravans
NEW WORLD REVIEW

Jan. 1968

ULAN BATOR, Peoples Republic of Mongolia,--- The thirteen year old girl in Ulan Bator did a fragile dance. Her bare arms were poised lightly, she swirled so the gold threads of her tunic caught and reflected the dazzling light. This, I said to myself, is the essence of Mongolia. Here, the liberation of the human spirit is embodied in the nimble feet of ten thousand dancing children. I turned to Damba, my interpreter. "What is her name?" I asked. He answered, "Selenga, the name of a river. Someday she will be a star."

Delegates from twenty-one countries to the Mongolian Youth Congress traveled across Siberia to Irkutsk. From there we crossed Lake Baikal southward above a range of snow-capped peaks , across the vast Mongolian steppe to Ulan Bator, the City of Caravans.

Ulan Bator (pop. 250,000) sprawls, looking from the air, somewhat like Butte, Montana, on the treeless, rolling steppe. Gay, pastel-colored, tall apartment buildings are intermingled with high cranes in the central area of the city. On the sides of a hill on the outskirts to the northeast is old-town. Enclosed by a wooden wall and dominated architecturally by the Buddhist Monastery at the summit. Here, thousands of people live in the hogan-like nomad felt tents called "gedas" by the Mongolians (known around the world as yurts).

"They are waiting their turn to move into the apartment houses," Damba told me as we drove from the airport to the hotel. "It won't be long."

I asked him if there are people in Mongolia who cherish the old way of life. He shook his head emphatically. "You will find on the contrary that everyone, even the old, are impatient for modern life. In fact, we who are youth leaders must warn the young people about being overhasty in abandoning the old practices."

The leader of the Youth League, Secretary Purewjaw, devoted time to this sharp appetite for the up-to-date when he spoke to the congress a day after we arrived in Ulan Bator, November 22 (1967). He said, "The youth hunger for education.....They hunger for the modern, socialist way of doing things."

The delegates engulfed me when I strolled into the foyer after his speech. Awkward looking young men in khaki military tunics, raven-haired women in apple-red and peach-colored silks crowded round to get their first glimpse of an American.

"I am from Aronghai province," one girl said. "I was elected because I am a champion sheep-herder. No lambs died in my flock because I was careful to bring them to the shelter when the wind blew hard. And I changed the bedding every day." I asked her how far it is from her farm to the next farm. My interpreter said, "She says it is 15 kilometers."

How did she come to Ulan Bator? Her face broke into a dazzling smile. By airplane. Was this her first trip? "Oh no. Many times. But first trip to Ulan Bator."

And what do young people do on your farm do on Saturday night? "We dance," she said. "We do the twist. It is our favorite." The band on their farm consists of a saxophone, a trumpet, two trombones, a clarinet, and drums, she proudly informed me. If they don't wish to dance, they go to a movie instead. Also we listen to the radio."

I told her I grew up on a dairy farm. "How many cows?" she asked. "Oh, my father milks about a hundred head," I answered. Her eyes grew large. "Very big!" Then she asked me about production. "A ton of milk each day," I told her. An excited buzz passed through the the onlookers as the figure was translated into kilograms.

"And do you use bulls for breeding purposes?" she asked. "No, we use artificial insemination." She nodded. "So do we. Soon we will buy a tractor. We want to plant wheat. Then a truck...."

@   @   @   @   @   @

Each night after dinner, in the columned dining room of our handsome hotel, Damba repeated the same question: "Coffee, Tea, or ice cream."

"Coffee," I would answer, though once I had tea for a change. "Who would take the offer of ice cream?" I thought, remembering the twenty degree below zero wind that was whistling its way out of Siberia and across the open steppe. Yet each night I was invited to try the ice cream.

Finally, in deference to my dairyman past, I accepted the offer of ice cream. It was brought to me in an elegant high stemmed silver Sundae dish and offered with a polite bow by the young waiter. Two cookies were thrust into the ice cream for decoration. I sampled a spoonful. I drew back. "Damba!," I exclaimed. "This is delicious. This is superb!"

I turned to my neighbors, the Frenchmen, and announced, "If you leave Mongolia without trying this ice cream, it will be a small tragedy.

"This," I announced categorically, "is the best ice cream in the world."

Damba beamed at me and shook his head in a futile effort to conceal his pleasure. "It is nothing. It is something new to us. We have no experience," he said.

And indeed it was the best ice cream in the world. Little nut-like flecks of vanilla beans were stirred into the mix, making this the most vanilla vanilla ice cream I ever tasted. Damba was translating my advice into Mongolian for the benefit of the Frenchmen's interpreter, Char. She laughed delightedly and called to the waiter. After that everyone tried Mongolian ice cream.

Why are they so sensitive to our reaction to these small details of hospitality? Why does it matter so much? The answer, I learned is to be found in the fact that Mongolia is an independent country. "When we make a mistake," Damba told me, "we have nobody to blame but ourselves. And when we do things right, then that is our triumph. It belongs to all of us." It would be a good thing, I thought to myself, if American young people could feel so intensely about the quality of a dish of ice cream!

@   @   @   @   @   @

"The Mongolian people have not always been so happy as you see they are now," said the young diplomat, Mr. Gundegma, as we strolled on a sunny afternoon in the national museum. Gundegma was a delicate young man with ascetic features and humorous eyes. He pointed to an ancient Buddhist silk screen painting of the five stages of spiritual perfection.

"Forty years ago, Mongolia was one of the most backward countrties in the world. Tens of thousands of Mongol men were Buddhist priests, beggars who impoverished the people. Our people were nomadic herdsmen who lived in cruel poverty. We had no native industry. For two hundreds years Mongolia was the victim of feudal warlords, the puppets of the Chinese warlords."

Then he gestured toward a heroic painting of a handsome young warrior mounted on horseback who beckoned over his shoulder to a mass of Mongol horseman behind him. "Here is Suche Bator, our national liberator. In 1921, he led the Mongolian people to national independence."

"He is so young," I remarked of the painting.

"He died in his early thirties," Gundegma said. "In forty years, we have come a long way. We are pioneers in an experiment of worldwide significance. We are building the technical base for socialism without passing through capitalism."

He told me that the Mongolian People's Republic (MPR) has a realistic plan for two-track development of the economy. The main stress lies on animal husbandry but a strong secondary stress is the building up of the industrial base.

"We are proud of the fact that Mongolia's relations with other countries are expanding. Mongolia is recognized by over fifty nations. We hope the USA will recognize the Mongolian People's Republic soon. Then we will exchange diplomats," he said, smiling.

I asked about relations with the USSR. "Of course, the Mongolian people have deep affection for the Soviet people because of the crucial aid they extended to us in our fight for national independence. Since then the USSR has extended great material aid to the MPR. You know that Red Army soldiers fought beside Mongolian troops against the Japanese army when they attempted to overrun Mongolia....."

And how about relations between the MPR and China? "We have great affection for the Chinese people," he said, "but recently difficulties have arisen." He told me about a woolen mill built in Ulan Bator with Chinese assistance. A few months previous to my visit, Gundegma said, the Chinese technical assistants in the mill began distributing anti-government leaflets in Ulan Bator accusing the Mongolian party of revisionism.

"They tried to organize street demonstrations against our Party," he added. The government had no choice but to expel the technicians from the country. I remembered, as Gundegma was speaking, that Damba had earlier told me some Chinese leaders believe Mongolia should be part of China.

"Now we are building apartment houses, hospitals, and schools. We can't keep up with the people's demands for the benefits of modern life," Gundegma said as we left the museum. He paused and weighed each word with emphasis. "That is why we must be realistic in our plan for socialist construction."

We visited Darkhan, City of Friendship, at the conclusion of the Congress. "This is Darkhan," the young mayor said, gesturing at the complex of fine new apartment houses. "We have built this city with the aid of the Soviet Union, Czechoslovakia, and Poland. Thirty thousand Mongolians live here where five years ago there was nothing but steppe."

We were shown the new elementary school with the most up-to-date architecture, comfortable desks and green chalkboards. We saw the nursery school wherte working mothers leave their children each day. We visited the clinic with gleaming stainless steel and fluorescent lighting and bustling Mongol doctors in white gowns.

"All this," the mayor said, "was built with the help of the Soviet Union, Czechoslovakia, and Poland." Even in winter, I observed, the playground was teeming with little children.

What a contrast, I thought to myself. The socialist countries build parks and playgrounds, apartment houses and clinics, schools and factories in Darkhan, City of Friendship.

But U.S. bombs are falling from Hanoi's skies to destroy schools, parks, apartment houses and playgrounds where the little children of Vietnam should be at play.

While the USSR is extending fraternal aid to raise the living standard of the Mongolian people, the USA is doing its utmost to destroy theVietnamese people's bid for national independence.

On the plane from Ulan Bator to Irkutsk as I was leaving Mongolia, I met a young woman. She was from the town of Hara. Her name was Chimidceren. She told me she was going to Leningrad to study at the agricultural institute. She said she was studying to become an orchardist and when her studies are completed, she would return to Hara and plant apple trees. Peace is apple trees blooming in Hara.

Joyce and I Fly to the Soviet Union

WASHINGTON—Alexander Evstafiev, First Secretary of the Soviet Embassy, visited my office in the National Press Building one morning in 1974. Aeroflot and Pan American Airways were inaugurating flights between Washington's Dulles Airport and Moscow's Sheremetyevo Airport in April. A delegation of dignitaries from the Nixon Administration was invited to fly on that first Aeroflot flight. The Embassy was extending an invitation to the *Daily World* to send someone as well.

I thanked him warmly and as soon as he left, telephoned the *DW* to convey the invitation. The word came back almost immediately: I should go.

But when I got home and delivered the news to Joyce, she had a warm response. "How about me? Can you arrange for me to go too?"

Next day, I walked over to the Soviet Embassy and met with Evstafiev. Within a couple of hours, word came back. Yes. Joyce was invited too.

The whirlwind trip included two days in Leningrad, three days in Moscow, and a visit, as well, to Kiev with many ceremonies and sightseeing at all three locations. This was my second visit to the USSR. The first was in 1967 on my way to Mongolia.

I remember the tears on Joyce's cheeks when we visited the children's "Pioneer Palace" in Kiev where we were greeted by a delegation of happy, healthy looking youngsters with red bandannas around their necks. Children, we were told, "are the only privileged class in the Soviet Union."

The large White House delegation included Transportation Secretary, Claude Brinegar, an oil millionaire with ice water—or crude oil—running in his veins. Several U.S. astronauts, including Dr. Joe Kerwin, commander of the U.S. space station were on the trip. Kerwin made several graceful toasts to our Soviet hosts, referring to his thoughts while flying aboard the space station of the imperative need for world peace as he looked down from the window at Planet Earth below.

We checked into the Intourist Hotel on Gorky Street, an easy walk from Red Square, when we first landed late at night on first arriving in the USSR.

I came down to the lobby next morning and beheld quite a remarkable sight. The entire lobby was filled with Nixon Administration officials all sitting in the lounge reading the most recent edition of the *Daily World*.

In those days, the Soviets purchased thousands of copies each day of the *Daily World* and distributed them to hotels throughout the USSR. It was prominently displayed among *Pravda*, *Izvestia*, *Trud* and other Soviet papers—all in Russia's Cyrillic alphabet. The *Daily World* was the most readable newspaper they could lay their hands on.

They were reading articles I and other *DW* staffwriters had written covering the vast popular movement against Nixon, Nixonomics, Nixon's war in Vietnam, and the "Third Rate Burglary" at the Watergate.

Joyce and I decided to take a stroll on Gorky Street. As we walked up the sidewalk, I saw an oddly familiar man coming up the stairs from the subway. I was stunned.... and so was he. It was Mike Davidow who had been our Moscow correspondent. He had no advance notice that I was on assignment covering that inaugural flight.

After completing his two year tour of duty in Moscow, Davidow had decided to stay in the USSR with his wife and their disabled son who was receiving treatment not available back in the U.S. We greeted each other like long lost brothers, embracing, pounding each other on the back and marveling at how small the world is. Mike remained permanently in the Soviet Union, covering the coup in 1990 that destroyed the USSR. He was unflinching in his defense of the first socialist revolution on earth. He died in Moscow.

Joyce and I were able to break free of the rigorous schedule to enjoy a delightful evening with the *Daily World's* correspondent, Joe North, and his wife Augusta. Joe sat at the upright piano and we sang hit songs composed by his brother, Alex: "Time goes by, so slowly and time can mean so much, are you still mine?"

Tourist in the USSR Join Shoppers
Daily World

April 26, 1974

WASHINGTON, April 25—While in Leningrad recently, a U.S. good-will delegation, which included this reporter and his wife, stayed at the aging but splendid Astoria Hotel just across from St. Isaacs Cathedral and a short walk from the Winter Palace.

"After the war, we found engraved invitations that the Nazis had prepared for a victory celebration at the Astoria Hotel" our Intourist guide Natasha gently informed us.

The Nazis at that time met with rude surprises. For us, though, all the surprises in a week of touring Leningrad, Kiev and Moscow were pleasant ones.

For most of us, it was our first visit to the Soviet Union. Others were avid, seasoned travelers in this immense land. All of us, however, found plenty to delight and surprise us, because the Soviet Union is undergoing such steady and remarkable change.

Even with the vestiges of winter still clinging to the cherry boughs in the orchards of the village of Pushkin near Leningrad, it was clear this is a land in bloom. Farm workers, on the day of our visit, were sinking a huge drainage system to carry off excess water from a vast marsh on the plains before Leningrad. On the horizon,

cranes loomed where men and women were construct-
ing apartment complexes to house thousands.

One week is not enough to see even the surface of reality in a country of such profound, revolutionary change.

Our tour, as guests of the Soviet Airline Aeroflot, was
organized on a moment-by-moment basis to jam as
much experience as possible into our brief stay.

Some of our most vivid impressions, nevertheless,
were gained during those precious moments when my
wife, Joyce, and I slipped off to explore on our own.

A walk in Kiev

On Krischatik Street in Kiev, men and women were
already up and about at 7:30 on a Sunday morning
when we set out for a walk. Food markets are open on
Sundays in the USSR and we strolled through a delica-
tessen store whose display cases were overflowing with
a dozen varieties of fragrant Ukrainian bread.

A stolid, ruddy-cheeked Ukrainian woman dressed in
dairy white was carving one-kilo chunks from a giant
block of fresh-churned butter. Nearby were piled big
round wheels of cheese.

Plump freshly plucked chickens and ducklings crowded
another refrigerated case, and beside this, a meat case
displayed ground beef and sausages. Succulent chunks
of beef slowly turned on a rotisserie. The clerks were
hastily preparing for an onslaught of customers.

Directly across the street, a long line stretched out of
the fish market where citizens were waiting to purchase
freshly caught bottom fish from the Dnieper River. Here
too, the display cases groaned with the silvery catch and
the air was pungent with the aroma of fresh fish.

A Moscow bakery

In Moscow we found the same copious supplies of food
and a few days later, during a two-hour walk through
shops on Gorky Street several blocks from Red Square.

A bakery in the Soviet Union occupies about the same space as a moderately large supermarket here in the U.S. There was the heavy, dense, sour-tasting black bread as well as ryes, pumpernickel, and white bread in long loaves.

The cities of the USSR are a feast for an artist's eyes. After all, it is more than eight centuries since Yuri Dolgoruky pointed his sword at the crest of a hill and decreed that a city (Moscow) would be built there.

Medieval cathedrals with their gilded onion domes coexist peacefully with modern structures in Moscow. The churches have been restored with loving care.

For all its rapid reconstruction, big parts of Moscow preserve a rugged frontier quality reminiscent of some western cities of the U.S. and Canada.

In the suburbs

In the suburbs, we found a village of wooden houses, their eves decorated with graceful wooden carvings. We saw a young woman in black boots, a bright peasant scarf around her face, cranking a bucket of water from the neighborhood well. Orchards with gnarled branches surrounded these weather-beaten houses and chickens foraged in the front yard.

Yet nearby, lofty cranes were rearing new apartments. In this country, where 34 million souls obtained new housing last year, entire cities have risen phoenix-like from the ashes of the war.

We visited the ancient monastery, Novodieveche, and one of our delegates was non-plussed to find hundreds of mostly elderly women worshiping at a Russian Ortho-dox Church.

"Wait a minute, I'm confused," he said. "I thought this was an atheistic country. I didn't think you could go to church."

This led to a discussion as we returned to our tour bus, of the decrees proclaimed by the Bolsheviks after the November 7, 1917 revolution abolishing religious persecution and guaranteeing freedom of worship. There was no religious freedom, no separation of church and state before the working class took power. Instead, there were bloody pogroms against the Jews—facts conveniently unreported in most U.S. classrooms today.

No slums or 'luxury'

What struck many in our delegation, including this reporter, most forcefully was the egalitarian quality of Soviet life. Nowhere in all the incredible building going on in Moscow can one find "luxury" housing. There are no mansions and there are no slum tenements.

People dressed warmly and well, but simply. True, Muscovites wear fur hats that would make the rich in the U.S. drool, but our bus driver was wearing such a "chapka."

We saw a prosperous country, a well-fed, well-dressed, visibly proud and hardworking people full of the fondest regard for the American people.

At a performance of Swan Lake in the Kremlin Palace of Congresses, one night, we sat beside a beautiful Soviet family—a young man, his wife and their son.

The boy spoke English, it turned out, and overcame his shyness when I pointed out the three U.S. Skylab astronauts sitting three rows back, members of our delegation.

Soviet youths hold their Cosmonauts in deep reverence as heroes and the child was clearly awed, as well, by the American spacemen. During the intermission, the astronauts autographed his ballet program and the boy, beaming his gratitude, autographed mine: "At the ballet, Swan Lake, Felix," he wrote.

His father spoke no English but succeeded in communicating to us that he is a "virologist" engaged in research at a Moscow scientific institute. He is a member of the Communist Party of the Soviet Union.

As we parted, he grasped my hand and broke into a torrent of fervent Russian, which I could not understand.

Perhaps he was telling us that human life on this planet depends on the cooperation of the U.S. and Soviet virologists in conquering diseases such as cancer.

Azerbaijan Women Discard Veil
Daily World

December 18, 1980

BAKU—With its curving bay and sandstone-colored houses rising on the hills to the north and west, Baku is surely one of the world's most beautiful cities. Olive trees, palms, cypress and oleander grow in the bayside park and here and there the skyline is broken by the domes of mosques and by soaring minarets. It is an ancient city, once the capital of the Shervanshah empire, and its palace has been carefully restored. A section of the old town, surrounded by a high stone wall, has been preserved. At the end of the narrow, cobblestone street in this old section is the "Caravanserai," built in the 16th century as a hostelry for caravan drivers who passed through Baku.

Now, it is a restaurant serving authentic Azerbaijanian cuisine in the vaulted, whitewashed cubicles that were once sleeping quarters. Beautiful oriental rugs are on the flagstone floor and walls and a band plays national songs. In the courtyard outside, guests perform authentic national dances of Azerbaijan. In this Asian republic the best of what is old is preserved.

Yet no sight in Baku moved us more than the tall, heroic statue on Gubanov Street, high on the crest of a hill overlooking the city, of an Azerbaijanian woman. She has just torn aside her veil, baring her proud face to the sun. The monument celebrates the liberation of Azerbaijanian women from feudal serfdom sixty years ago with the final victory of Soviet power. On our second day in Baku, we went to "Order of the Red Banner School Number 190" and met Tageava Sona, principal of this celebrated institution which teaches reading, writing, math, science, social studies and the arts to classes one through ten.

Mrs. Tageava Sona has lived through the entire period of Soviet power and played such a crucial role in the struggle against oppression of women and against mass illiteracy, that she was awarded the "Order of Lenin," the highest decoration of the Soviet Union this past October 4. Standing beneath a portrait of Lenin in her simply furnished office and smoothing her gray hair as she spoke, Mrs. Sona told us her life struggle against illiteracy. "When Soviet power was being established, it was very hard for a young woman to get an education," she said. "I was the oldest in my family and I was chosen to go to school. But there was a big commotion. My father was opposed. My aunt worked hard to convince him to allow me to go—and so I did.

"I had been working at this school for thirty years and one day, my father was listening to the radio and he heard a report that I had been elected to the Supreme Soviet of Azerbaijan. He almost cried with happiness that his child, his daughter was being honored. I am still a deputy of the Supreme Soviet and a deputy of Baku City Soviet. I am an 'honored teacher' of the Azerbaijan Republic.

"The children of the children I taught to read and write are now sending their children to this school so I can say all the pupils here are my grandchildren."

Mrs. Sona led us on a tour of the classrooms where first graders and second graders recited poems solo or in unison.

"I'm a little girl . . . I go to school . . . I never met Lenin but I love him," said one tiny little person with jet black pigtails.

Language school

This is an Azerbaijan language school, meaning that Russian is taught as the second language. Children throughout the republic have their choice of attending Russian language schools or of attending schools in their own language. About eighty percent of Azerbaijanian children attend Azerbaijanian language schools.

We entered a third grade classroom, filled with sunlight and potted plants on the window sills, to find the children studying Farsi, the language of Iran, whose border is less than 200 miles from Baku. "What do you want to be when you grow up?" I asked one little boy. "I want to be a linguist," he promptly replied through our interpreter.

We toured the ninth grade physics and chemistry lab where a teacher was explaining vector analysis with a graph on the blackboard. The lab was fully equipped with weights and measures, a hood, and lab tables with sinks and gas lines for Bunsen burners. As many girls were enrolled in the physics class as boys.

Mrs. Sona said goodbye to us in her office. "Our great dream is that friendship between our two countries will grow stronger," she said.

High birth rate

Earlier, we visited Elmira Kafarova, a young woman, formerly a leader of the Young Communist League, and now Minister of Education for the Republic of Azerbaijan. She warmly greeted us and invited us onto her spacious office at Government House. Azerbaijan, she said, has one of the highest birth rates of the fifteen Soviet Republics and education is therefore a high priority.

In 1914, she said, only 23,000 Azerbaijanian children were enrolled in 960 mostly one room Islamic schools throughout the country. Illiteracy was well over ninty-five percent.

"Now, we have 4,000 schools with an enrollment of 1.4 million children. Most of our schools have grades one through ten. We have 110,000 elementary and secondary school teachers. The first decree after the victory of the revolution was on 'Free, Universal Education,'" she said.

"Our educational system seeks to develop in each student a harmonious personality and dedication to world peace."

A basic concept in the education of youth is preparation for a "life career."

"As you know, the technical revolution is developing very fast and we must prepare our youth to fully participate in this revolution. That is why we are providing more and more hours in our schools for higher technical skills."

At the time of the revolution, she concluded, "women lacked many rights. Religion suppressed the development among girls of reading, writing, mathematics, music and literature. Now we can look back on sixty years of development of our schools in Azerbaijan," she concluded.

McCarthyism German-style
People's Weekly World

The following is the second in a series of articles by *People's Weekly World* editor Tim Wheeler on his trip to Germany early last month.

November 26, 1994
BERLIN, Germany—In seizing the property of 16 million citizens of the former German Democratic Republic (GDR) and subjecting east Germans to second class citizenship, Chancellor Helmut Kohl faces a problem: how to justify it in the eyes of world public opinion.

Most of this property was built from the ruins of World War II by the people of the GDR. The Treaty of Unification embraces the legal formula, "restitution before compensation." It means that wealthy corporations and landlords, many of them Nazis and Nazi sympathizers, whose property had been socialized by the GDR, could now reclaim their property and this would take priority over any compensation for citizens of the GDR. So far, more than 2.3 million claims, mostly by west Germans, have been filed.

But what about entirely new factories and industries that were built since the GDR was founded in 1949? The

Kohl regime's strategy has been to portray this property as obsolete and practically worthless. The government agency set up to privatize the GDR economy, called the Treuhand Agency, has auctioned it at fire sale prices.

They served the GDR

The bottom line is that east Germans are dispossessed and increasingly angry. It is reflected in the stunning vote for the Party of Democratic Socialism (PDS) last October 16 which sent thirty PDS candidates to the Bundestag.

Kohl's answer to this strong left rebound has been to intensify a witch hunt that targets more than 250,000 people for the "crime" of having served Germany's first socialist state. Already, tens of thousands of school teachers have been blacklisted. Also targeted are all judges and prosecutors, border troops, military and state security officers (the so-called Stasi), leaders of the GDR's ruling Socialist Unity Party, soldiers and police officers.

The witch hunt includes high profile trials like those of General Heinz Kessler, General Fritz Strelitz, Markus Wolf and others, some of whom are now in prison. This "McCarthyism German-style" is a perfect cover to confiscate property of a state that has been branded "unlawful."

Victims of the witch hunt are being defended by several solidarity groups. Hans Reichert is chair of the Committee for Humanitarian Assistance (CHA). He was the former Deputy Prime Minister of the GDR and leader of the Democratic Peasants Party. "Anyone who dared to defend and work for the success of the GDR must be punished," he told me through an interpreter. "They seek to criminalize the very idea of socialism. They never condemned the General Staff of the fascist army after 1945. It was not declared a 'criminal organization.' But Klaus Kinkel, former head of the west German intelligence service, recently declared, 'We must de-legitimize the GDR.'"

Hans Bauer, former Deputy Attorney General of the GDR, serves as a CHA attorney. He cited the case of GDR intelligence officer Markus Wolf, who was convicted of treason. He is free on appeal "It is ridiculous," said Bauer. "These intelligence officers never betrayed their socialist homeland! Markus Wolf was not employed by the Federal German Republic. He served the GDR."

Nightmares of McCarthy

"We remember what happened to people in the United States during the McCarthy era," Bauer continued. "There are many similarities— indictments, trials, and blacklists of people for cynical political motives."

In the final negotiations on unification, the Kohl regime made a promise that it would push a no-reprisal law through the Bundestag, to prohibit retribution against officials who had acted according to GDR laws and policies in defending the territory of the socialist state. The logic of such a law was that the unification brought together two sovereign states, with the explicit recognition of the lawfulness of both.

Kohl's conservative coalition government introduced the no-reprisal law, but it was blocked by the Social Democratic Party, as if in an orchestrated setup. The witch hunt is resounding proof that this was no unification of equal sovereign states but rather a forced annexation of the GDR. It is now treated as conquered territory, its officials hunted like criminals. But west Germany engaged in espionage and acts of covert warfare against the GDR and the perpetrators are not being prosecuted, even in cases that involved assassination and murder of GDR border troops.

Mass indoctrination

"This is aimed at the masses of the people," said Reichert. "The West German state took over 16 million GDR citizens who were profoundly educated in an anti-fascist and anti-capitalist spirit. Socialism sank deep roots in the minds of our people. For the capitalist regime in Bonn, this socialist consciousness is like a cancer that must be cut out." Thus, one aim of the Kohl regime, similar to McCarthyism, is to foster a stoolpigeon mentality, informing on your fellow workers as well as self-denunciation. Stasi files are used and manipulated for frame-up purposes. "This witch hunt is above all mass indoctrination—brainwashing," Reichert said. "To defend General Kessler and the other targets of this witch hunt is to defeat this brainwashing."

The main objective of the CHA, he continued, is to give all possible legal and moral support for all victims of persecution. The second goal is to build a broad-based, non-partisan movement against political repression. So far, the CHA has 1,200 members and is growing steadily in all parts of east Germany, as victims and their supporters begin to fight back.

Several other solidarity groups have affiliated with the CHA, including the former Erich Honecker Defense Committee, now renamed the Solidarity Committee (SC). It is based in west Berlin where I met one afternoon with the group's leaders. Chair Klaus Feske said international solidarity is a high priority. They have sent out an international appeal and have received many positive replies.

In a letter, Baron Maurice Goldstein, president of the International Auschwitz Committee, declared his group's support. "There is an urgent necessity for an organized reaction against the measures of intimidation and threats," he declared. The Dachau Committee also sent an endorsement. An anti-fascist group in the Netherlands sent a letter of protest to west German prosecutor, Roman Herzog. "The Dutch people have an enormous hatred of the Nazis, and if things go on as they are now, they will hate the government of Federal Germany as well," the letter warned. Members of the SC had just returned from a meeting in Paris with a committee that collected tens of thousands of petition signatures demanding release of Honecker who was imprisoned at that time.

Packing the courtrooms

Ruth Kessler, the wife of General Heinz Kessler, is a member of the SC. "I feel that Heinz and the others are not in jail at this time only because of this committee's struggles," she told me. "We were able to fill the courtroom every day for sixty-eight days of his trial. The judge and the public prosecutor were tremendously irritated." Kessler was sentenced to seven-and-one-half years in prison, but is free on appeal.

The members of the SC stressed the underlying motives of the witch hunt. "It is revenge for the role played by the GDR in blocking German imperialism's great power ambitions for forty years," said Werner Engst, who had been responsible for youth work and education in the GDR. "They can never forgive us for the role we played in pushing up wages and benefits for workers in west Germany. Whenever west German workers sat down to negotiate with their employers, there was a third silent partner sitting at the workers' side—the GDR."

Supplying cheap labor

Many of the benefits won with the help of the GDR are under attack by west German banks and corporations now that the GDR is gone, Engst said. A huge wage differential means that west German workers are being terminated from their jobs, replaced by east Germans as well as other eastern European workers desperate for a job even at starvation wages. German monopoly is cunningly playing all workers against each other to wring super-profits from their labor, he said.

Heinz Geggel, a former leader of the Socialist Unity Party, told me, "As a state, Germany has completed its unity. But in reality, the gulf between the two Germanys is deeper than ever. Socialism penetrated all parts of life of human beings in the GDR in ways west Germany never considered. Now many people in both the east and the west recognize that what happened was a betrayal."

Geggel continued, "Unemployment is high, not only in the east but also in the west. Many social achievements of the GDR have been totally demolished, but in the west, too, the Kohl regime is forcing through heavy reductions of social rights and benefits. It is a part of the ultra-conservative course to be observed, not only in Germany but all over Europe and the world." Kohl blames it all on the GDR. It is his scapegoat. "We must convince people to fight on our side—not only socialists and Communists, but trade unionists, religious people, and all others who will suffer losses from this witch hunt."

The Other Israel: Hava Keller, Champion of Palestinian Women
People's Weekly World

August 2, 1997

TEL AVIV—It is hard to imagine this soft-spoken grandmother, Hava Keller, as an infantry soldier in Israel's Haganah armed forces during the 1948 war of independence. But Keller told me during an interview at the seaside Shalom Hotel here that the war turned her into a lifelong activist for peace and justice.

She is now the leader of the Committee for Women Political Prisoners and has worked to build solidarity with Palestinian women for the past ten years.

"I was an ordinary combat soldier, not an officer," she said, recalling the events of 1948. "I was among the soldiers who conquered the town of Acco (Acre). We entered a house that belonged to an Arab family."

The residents had fled. The table was set for breakfast. "I looked down and there on the floor was a pair of child's shoes. I said to myself, 'They left his shoes! He'll get cold!'"

There were many things worse than that that happened during the war, but that moment made a deep impression on her.

"I said to myself, 'It should not be done this way.' I hoped that the war would end soon and we would live in peace. I never imagined that people would be driven from their homes and never allowed to return."

Keller was born in Poland and emigrated to Palestine in 1941. All of her family who remained in Europe died in the Nazi concentration camps.

"From the Holocaust, you can come to two conclusions," she told me. "It should never again happen to anyone or it should never again happen to us."

Her position is clear. "It should never again happen to anyone. The plight of the Palestinians is not the same as the Holocaust, but it is bad enough!"

Keller spent her early years in Palestine on a kibbutz. Later, after the war, she completed her studies and became a high school teacher of history and civics. "Our children's education in Israel was so narrow. I was determined to broaden it. I taught courses in Islamic history and culture that were very popular with the students. The administration tried to fire me and my students came to my defense." She taught for more than thirty years before she retired.

She was galvanized into action in 1988 by the Intifada, the mass uprising of Palestinian youth in occupied Gaza and the West Bank. "It was a shock," she said. "Here were Palestinian children fighting with stones against heavily armed Israeli soldiers. We knew we had to do something."

A Palestinian woman came to Keller with a terrible story. Israeli soldiers had broken into a Palestinian home in the Gaza Strip and abducted a woman, Aisha El Kurd who was eight months pregnant with her fourth child. The children were left in the care of the children's paralyzed grandmother while soldiers threw Aisha on the floor of a jeep and drove her at high speeds on unpaved roads evidently with the intention of inducing a miscarriage.

Finally they delivered her to prison where labor pains started. Her fellow inmates demanded that she be taken to the hospital. After she gave birth she was returned to prison.

"Her husband pleaded for her release," Keller said. "He told the Israeli authorities he would confess to anything if only they would release her. So the judge agreed that she would be released if she paid $3,000 U.S. currency—it is much better than shekels."

Keller said, "We ran like crazy from one end of Israel to the other to raise money for her release." They succeeded and Aisha was released but there was no place for her to go because the Israeli authorities had bulldozed her home.

"The United Nations gave her a tent. We made collections for her all over the world and bought her a home. We helped her get training as a midwife," Keller said. "Now she lives with her children in Gaza and somehow manages to eke out a living. Her husband is still in prison."

The movement was struggling to win justice for an estimated 5,000 Palestinian women. "Nobody knows exactly how many Palestinian women are imprisoned but we know there are more than 300 'administrative detainees,' some of them in jail since 1992," Keller said.

These "administrative detainees" have not been tried or convicted of any crime but are simply held indefinitely in the extensive network of prisons scattered throughout Israel. (During my travels across the Israeli countryside, I counted seven of these ramshackle prisons, their walls topped with concertina wire and guard towers at every corner).

Keller and her committee played an important role in the struggle to free thirty-four Palestinian women prisoners, a battle that became so intense that their release was written into the so-called Oslo II agreement signed by PLO Leader Yassir Arafat and Israeli Prime Minister Yitzhak Rabin at the Hilton-Taba Hotel on Egypt's Red Sea coast September 25, 1995. Implementation of the 400-page agreement was guaranteed by the Clinton administration.

Two months later, Rabin was assassinated by a right-wing extremist after speaking to a peace rally of 100,000 people in Tel Aviv. As for the imprisoned Palestinian women, they continued to languish in Tel-Mond prison.

Keller made a pilgrimage every week to the jail outside Netanya where they were incarcerated. She got to know each of the women's families and her committee ended up serving as liaison with the inmates and the outside world.

Four months after Oslo II was signed, the Israelis still had not released the women. "It was written very clearly in Oslo II that all the women prisoners and detainees were to be released at once," Keller said. "The Israeli government was ready to release twenty-five of them but the remaining prisoners were not to be released."

In January 1995, the Palestinian women revolted. When the Israeli authorities attempted to release only the twenty-five women, they rushed into one tiny cell and barricaded themselves.

"All would leave the prison, or none would leave," said Keller. "They started a hunger strike and announced that if the prison authorities stormed the cell, they would all kill themselves."

The hunger strike lasted twenty-one days. But in the beginning, no one on the outside knew it was happening. Then one of the women managed to slip a note to one of the criminal inmates who had telephone privileges. The note said, "Call Hava Keller" with her phone number. The inmate did.

"She told me everything," Keller said. "At once, I telephoned the TV and radio stations and told them to send reporters because something interesting was happening at Tel-Mond prison."

The prison was besieged by scores of broadcast and print journalists and the story was out. (The *People's Weekly World* carried a report by our Middle East correspondent, Hans Lebrecht, on February 10, 1996). The peace movement mobilized and Netanyahu was compelled to release all the women.

Yet even as the victory was unfolding, Keller and her women's committee played a crucial role. She telephoned a leader of the Palestinian Liberation Organization at PLO headquarters in Gaza and asked him to fax her their list of the inmates.

"As soon as it came through, I went over it and found they had only twenty-seven names," she said. "If they had submitted that list to the Israeli government, several of the women might be left in prison. So I faxed a message back to the PNA adding the missing names."

On the day of the release, Keller was in the crowd that gathered at the prison gate. "The PLO leader was also there. He spotted me standing at the fence and came running to kiss me. It was a victory!" Of course, she added, hundreds of Palestinian men remain imprisoned in Israel and the battle to free them is an urgent, unfinished task.

The weekend before I arrived in Israel, Keller and her committee helped organize a demonstration of over 1,000 Palestinian Arab and Israeli women through the streets of Jerusalem.

They carried banners that proclaimed, "Jerusalem is an undivided city - and the capital of two states, Israel and Palestine." It was one of the most dramatic actions yet of a growing phenomenon, Arabs and Jews demonstrating together for a just peace. "It was a joint demonstration initiated by two organizations, Bat Shalom and Jerusalem Links. We were very pleased because quite a few men marched with us," Keller said.

Joint actions are now growing in effectiveness, she said, since Gush Shalom (Peace Bloc) launched a petition drive calling for peace. "Quite a few people, both Israeli and Palestinian signed. It included the son of the current mayor of Jerusalem and the brother of Netanyahu's wife," she said, with a merry twinkle in her blue eyes.

Many of the joint demonstrations are organized on the spur of the moment to protest the Israeli settlers who seek to grab Palestinian land—at Jhalad Abu Ghneim (Har Homa), a hill midway between Jerusalem and Bethlehem, for example, where Israeli bulldozers have cleared a forest from the hillside to make way for a Jewish settlement.

"The Palestinians are angry and we stand with them. The only possibility of living as human beings for both Israelis and Palestinians is to live in peace. The alternative is war - and then there will be a terrible stillness here," she said.

"I have two grandchildren, I don't want them to die," Keller said. "I'm not happy about nationalistic states. But without a state of their own, the Palestinians will simply be swallowed. They must have a state and gain economic, social and cultural strength."

It was late at night, the eve of my departure from Israel when the interview was over, but Keller told me she had more work at her office. I asked her how she would get there this late at night.

"Oh, I travel everywhere by bus," she said. So we walked together through Tel Aviv's darkened streets to her bus stop. I kissed her on her cheek when we said good-bye.

'Si, Se Puede'
The Cuban people defend their revolution
People's Weekly World

Dec. 14, 1996.
HAVANA—After five years of belt-tightening and self-sacrifice to save their revolution, the Cuban people finally see signs of a dawn. The economy is once again growing after the collapse of the Soviet Union destroyed eight-five percent of Cuba's export market, a blow that struck the

View of Almandares, Havana. From an original oil pastel by author

island with a force of ten hurricanes. Washington saw it as their chance, finally, to finish off Cuban socialism.

They enacted the Torricelli bill and the Helms-Burton bill to tighten the thirty-four-year economic blockade, an act of war that still inflicts pain and suffering on the Cuban people. Jorge Mas Canosa and his Miami mafia were already packing their bags for a triumphant return to Havana.

Their plans haven't panned out.

Juan Triana Cordovi, director of the Center for the study of the Cuban Economy, told me Cuba's 450,000 sugar cane workers are expected to harvest five million tons of sugar this year—double the tonnage during the depths of the "special period." The nickel miners have already produced 50,000 tons of refined nickel and cobalt in a joint venture with Sherritt International, the Canadian corporation that refuses to bow to Senator Jesse Helms. Joint ventures in tourism and other industries are bringing in development capital.

It is all the result of the determined hard work by millions of Cuban workers and campesinos. They process the indomitable spirit of the *Old Man and the Sea.*

Everywhere I visited during a one-week tour of Havana and nearby cities, this month, I saw signs of material shortages inflicted by the blockade. And everywhere I witnessed the quiet determination not to "say uncle" to Washington's pressure tactics. Two slogans can be seen on walls and buildings everywhere: "Si se puede!" (Yes we can do it!) and "Patria o Muerte" (Fatherland or death.)

Crowds wait with the patience of Job at bus stops. Every imaginable conveyance has been pressed into service, even ox carts. Hundreds of 1950s era Chevies trundle along, most of them running on hand-made spare parts. Soviet motorcycles with sidecars carry as many as five passengers.

The Cubans have invented the "camel," a semi-trailer with two humps pulled by a truck. Passengers are packed in like sardines. Thousands ride the Chinese-manufactured bicycles, hitchhike, or walk. There are similar chronic problems with fitful elevators, water, electricity, and telephone service.

The "si se puede" spirit may be part of the Cuban character—but it is also organized by grassroots leaders like Maria Ducas Megret. In March 1993, Cuba held its first elections for municipal and national "Assemblies of People's' Power." Maria Ducas Megret was elected to both the Municipal Assembly in Havana and the National Assembly representing the Marianao munici-pality, a neighborhood in west Havana where she lives.

"Our aim was to create a structure that would be closer to the population so that we could be more effec-tive in helping solve the problems faced by the people," she said as she led my interpreter and me on a walking tour of her district.

Judging by the reception Ducas received from her constituents, Cuba's brand of grassroots democracy is working well. Everyone seems to know her and rushed to embrace her.

Dominating Marianao is a sprawling former military base, the Columbia Fortress, built by the U.S. after the defeat of Spain in 1898. When Cuba's Revolutionary Army liberated Havana in January 1959, this was dictator Fulgencio Batista's last stronghold.

After it fell, the fort was renamed Ciudad Libertad (Freedom City.) The barracks were converted into schools, a newly constructed pediatric hospital, day care centers and a senior citizens center. Also located here is a teacher's college and Cuba's School of Fine Arts.

The afternoon we visited, it was teeming with children enjoying after-school programs—sports, art, music and dance. Some children were demonstrating their skills with watercolors and pastels. Others were working with clay fashioning plates and bowls. A chorus of Young Pioneers sang patriotic songs and performed group dances.

Gretel Gil, twelve, showed me the plate she had made with an excellent likeness of José Marti glazed into its surface. "José Marti made speeches in Tampa and New York City calling for Cuba's independence," she told me. "He died fighting for freedom because we were ruled first by Spain and then the U.S."

Maria Ducas took us to a residential neighborhood in Marianao where a group of volunteers, with the assistance of an architect and journeyman construction workers, built their own cinderblock apartment building, the Pilar House. Materials to construct the house were provided by the government.

The housing shortage is so acute that every one of the eight apartments is already furnished, decorated and occupied. The roof is a spacious patio that commands a panorama of the entire neighborhood. People from throughout Havana are now coming to learn the Marianao brigade's building methods. We walked two blocks to the home of Rita Rios, another neighborhood activist. It was after dark by now but the house was packed with community residents who had gathered to welcome me. It included artists who use the Rio home as an art gallery and children who are studying dance at a neighborhood ballet school.

Several years ago, Rios learned that the celebrated Cuban artist Winifredo Lam had lived in her home from 1941 to 1945 and had painted some of his greatest masterpieces there. Rios launched a campaign to restore the house.

Residents have joined in the campaign—typical of the type of grassroots initiative the "Assemblies of People's Power" seeks to stimulate. "The revolution gave me this house and I decided that I must give something back," Rios told me. "I am a revolutionary."

Havana's Spanish-style mansions date as early as the 16th century. They are decorated with fluted marble columns, ornate lintels and arches, wrought iron, stained glass and graceful porticos. The beauty is compounded by the lush semi-tropical vegetation—palm trees, blooming hibiscus and bougainvillea.

The climate is so balmy that few houses have glass windows. Most are fitted with louvered shutters. Open them and soft breezes warmed by the Gulf stream flow through the houses on a November afternoon. Yet many of Havana's lovely dwellings are crumbling because of shortages of building materials.

Here, too, I found a determined fightback. I went to the Maqueta de la Capital (Model of the Capital) in the Miramar municipality of Havana. This is a vast room-sized model of the city, which enables the people to get a bird's-eye view of their city. Miguel Coyula, an architect who works with the Group for Reconstruction of the Capital, a designer of the model, told me they are drawing up a plan for the restoration of the city, in part to make Havana a premier destination for tourism.

"Havana is a living museum," he told me. "The elite did not destroy their homes to build new ones. They simply abandoned them and moved further west. Now they live in Florida. So all the architectural monuments of the past are still standing, ready to be restored."

Already, construction has begun in Old Havana. "Part of my job is liaison with neighborhoods, to encourage the

people who live there to join in the effort to restore their communities."

I told him we had just visited Wifredo Lam's house in Marianao. "Oh," he exclaimed, his eyes brightening. "Did you meet Maria Ducas? She is wonderful! The Wifredo Lam house is the kind of restoration project we are trying to encourage."

I traveled to the Antero Regalado cooperative farm near San Antonio de los Baños where Israeli-designed cultivation houses are used to produce big succulent tomatoes—part of the drive to dramatically increase the supply of vegetables for Cuba's booming tourist industry. Here, too, the "Si se puede" principal was in force.

There are no spare parts for the cooperative's fleet of aging Soviet tractors. Nivalbo Ortega, president of the co-op, showed me the machine shop with an aging turret lathe, drill press, and other machine tools where they manufacture spare parts. "Before the revolution, we had millions of hectares of land that served only the needs of the wealthy," he told me. "Now our task is to guarantee a balanced diet for the Cuban people."

The 283-hectare co-op with 140 members produces vegetables that are sold to Acopio, the state agricultural marketing monopoly, for distribution. Some of the tomatoes are earmarked for the restaurants in Cuba's spanking new hotels—part of the integrated economic complex to serve Cuba's new tourist industry.

That Saturday before my departure, I was driven 100 miles east to Varadero Beach, its white sandy peninsula curving for miles into the Florida Gulf. Warmed by the Gulf stream, the waters are a brilliant turquoise blue.

The DuPont family once owned much of Varadero and their mansion is still standing. But the commanding presence in Varadero today is the Cuban Communist Party. A big sign on the façade of the modern party headquarters proclaims "Patria o Muerte."

Armando Castañeda and Osmany Almeida, two regional Party leaders, are assigned to oversee this bold foray into joint ventures with foreign corporations. Spanish, Italian, German, French, Canadian and Mexican corporations have flocked to Varadero. Jointly with Cuba they have built a necklace of five-star luxury hotels along Varadero Beach that are now filling up with thousands of tourists from Canada, Latin America and Europe.

So far, 8,000 hotel rooms have been completed by 10,000 Cuban construction workers. Another 20,000 workers are employed in other parts of the tourist industry in Varadero. Profits are split fifty-fifty and Cuba retains ultimate ownership of the properties.

"DuPont owned much of this and now the DuPonts are claiming it under the Helms-Burton law," said Castañeda with a chuckle. "The U.S. is losing, of course. The longer the blockade exists, the more behind they get. When they awake from their dreams, there won't be any space left for joint ventures with U.S. companies."

It is not possible to take the measure of a nation and its people in one brief week. Yet there were so many poignant impressions I took home with me. I did not hear a single angry exchange between Cubans in the streets despite all the obvious hardships they face.

Cuba is a remarkably multiracial society with Black, white and brown peoples living and working side-by-side. There is none of the racist segregation that divides our neighborhoods and schools. Pedro Ross Leal, a Cuban of African descent, is the president of the Cuban Labor Federation, a member of the ruling Council of State (equivalent to a cabinet minister.) He granted me an interview and then took me to a celebration of the 35th anniversary of the founding of Cuba's Public Employees Union.

As we entered the meeting hall, he handed me a lapel button. It read, "Yo creo en la solidaridad" (I believe in solidarity.) The buttons had been sent by a sister union in Puerto Rico. Solidarity seems to be a way of life in Cuba and a big rock in the way of those who would destroy the Cuban people's power.

Chapter 5

Mean Streets, Kindly Streets

A Baltimore "Arabber" with his little Assateague horse and buckboard loaded with fruits and vegetables trundles down the kindly inner city streets on a warm August afternon. He sings loudly, "Sweet straaawberries, cantaloupes, wateeermelon, tomaaatoes."(from an original watercolor by the author)

CIA LINKED TO SPYING BY LOCAL POLICE DEPTS.

By Tim Wheeler
Daily World

BALTIMORE, March 11 (1975)---Rep. Parren Mitchell (D-MD) charged today that a Baltimore police department spy plot against more than 125 citizen organizations, including the Baltimore-Washington AFL-CIO, is part of a "nationwide CIA apparatus."

LIBRARY
MAR 19 1975
UNIVERSITY OF
WASHINGTON

15¢

DAILY WORLD

CONTINUING the DAILY WORKER, FOUNDED 1924

Wednesday
Mar. 12
1975

Vol. VII, No. 167   New York, N.Y.   Daily except Sun., Mon. and major holidays

CIA LINKED TO SPYING BY LOCAL POLICE DEPTS.

Rockefeller puts lid on CIA murder facts
See page 3

Portugal rebuffs barracks provocation
See page 3

The Hawkins-Reuss full employment bill
See page 6

By TIM WHEELER

BALTIMORE, March 11 — Rep. Parren Mitchell (D-Md) charged today that a Baltimore police department spy plot against more than 125 citizen organizations, including the Baltimore-Washington AFL-CIO is part of a "nationwide CIA apparatus."

Baltimore has been rocked in recent months by disclosures of the spy operation carried out by the so-called Inspectional Services Division (ISD) of the Baltimore Police Department. The spying was done under orders from Police Commissioner Donald Pomerleau, an appointee of Gov. Marvin Mandel.

The plot involves infiltration of the groups by ISD agents, illegal break-ins, burglary, electronic surveillance and direct personal intimidation by Pomerleau.

Recent charges of CIA involvement in domestic spying, break-ins and assassinations abroad and possibly even in the U.S. have spotlighted the wide extent of the spy plot here.

Annapolis plot

Several former ISD agents have surfaced to testify at a Maryland State Senate investigation of the plot in Annapolis amid growing demands that Pomerleau be fired and that Congress investigate the plot.

Rep. Mitchell today requested the Justice Department and the U.S. Senate Committee headed by Sen. Frank Church (D-Idaho)

who are probing domestic CIA spying, to investigate the situation in Baltimore.

A top secret ISD memo released to the press recently listed the names of 125 organizations targeted for spying and disruption, including virtually every prominent Black, political, religious and civic leader in the city.

The list included the Black Ministerial Alliance, the NAACP, Operation Breadbasket, SCLC, the American Civil Liberties Union, SANE, Women's International League for Peace and Freedom, Interfaith Peace Committee, etc.

First on the list was the Communist Party of Maryland.

The Young Workers Liberation League and the Baltimore Free Angela Davis Committee were also targets.

Anti-Klan protesters listed

The ISD also kept dossiers on Baltimore citizens who came to the defense of the New Era Book shop when it was firebombed by the Ku Klux Klan several years ago.

The Baltimore Sun disclosed last month that the Baltimore Police Department kept files on all citizens who wrote to the editor of the Sun protesting the KKK violence.

The Sun also revealed that a fierce battle had raged between the then Baltimore Mayor Theodore McKeldin and Pomerleau over the request for police protection for the bookshop which specializes in Marxist, Black liberation, peace and working-class literature.

Pomerleau wanted to give the bookshop and the nazis the green light for destroying the bookshop but McKeldin, according to the Sun, ordered him to assign police to protect the shop.

Strikebreaking device

A separate police department memo revealed that the Baltimore-Washington AFL-CIO was a top priority target of ISD spying which became particularly intense last spring as Mandel and Pomerleau attempted to break militant strikes in Baltimore by sanitation workers, teachers and police.

'Not Isolated'

"I don't think you can treat it in isolation, it is part of the nationwide apparatus," Mitchell

REP. PARREN MITCHELL

told the Daily World today. "I definitely ties in with the CIA. We can document that the local ISD sent information to the CIA and the FBI and that these sent information back to ISD.

"I have already written to Church's committee. I told them their investigation of CIA domestic spying will be incomplete unless they look at the role of local police departments as part of the CIA apparatus."

Mitchell said that a request he sent to the Justice Department for an investigation of the ISD plot had been forwarded to the Justice Department's civil rights division.

Previous dirty tricks

Rep. Mitchell said he had suspected for years that CIA "dirty tricks" had been used against progressive movements in Baltimore. He recalled a confrontation between Black leaders and Pomerleau in 1971 at the offices of the Baltimore Afro-American newspaper, when Pomerleau boasted, "I know when you meet, I know what you plan in your meetings, I know before you meet."

Mitchell added, "Black leaders were spied on, bugged, followed and reported on until sufficient information was gained to intimidate

Continued on page 7

JOIN BROOKLYN COALITION

Rally held last month by Brooklyn Coalition to Fight Inflation and Unemployment. The group has called a meeting for March 19 to discuss the April 26 mass demonstration for jobs. See page 2.

Baltimore has been rocked in recent months by disclosures of a spy operation carried out by the so-called Inspectional Services Division (ISD) of the Baltimore Police Department. The spying was done under orders from Police Commissioner, Donald Pomerleau, an appointee of Gov. Marvin Mandel.

The plot involves infiltration of the groups by ISD agents, illegal break-ins, burglary, electronic surveillance, and direct personal intimidation by Pomerleau.

Recent charges of CIA involvement in domestic spying, break-ins and assassinations abroad, and possibly even in the U.S. have spotlighted the extent of the spy plot here.

Several former ISD agents have surfaced to testify at a Maryland State Senate investigation of the plot in Annapolis amid growing demands that Pomerleau be fired and that Congress investigate the plot.

Rep. Mitchell today requested the Justice Department and the U.S. Senate Committee headed by Sen. Frank Church (D-Idaho), who are probing domestic CIA spying, to investigate the situation in Baltimore.

A top secret ISD memo released to the press recently listed the names of 125 organizations targeted for spying and disruption, including virtually every prominent Black political, religious, and civic leader in the city.

The list included the Black Ministerial Alliance, the NAACP, Operation Breadbasket, SCLC, the American Civil Liberties Union, SANE, Women's International League for Peace and Freedom, Interfaith Peace Committee, etc.

First on the list was the Communist Party of Maryland.

The Young Workers Liberation League and the Baltimore Free Angela Davis Committee were also targets.

The ISD kept dossiers on Baltimore citizens who came to the defense of the New Era Bookshop when it was firebombed by the Ku Klux Klan several years ago. The *Baltimore Sun* disclosed last month that the Baltimore Police Department kept files on all citizens who wrote to the editor of the Sun protesting the KKK violence.

The *Sun* also revealed that a fierce battle had raged between the then Baltimore Mayor, Theodore McKeldin and Pomerleau over the request for police protection for the bookshop which specializes in Marxist, Black liberation, peace, and working class literature.

Pomerleau wanted to give the Klan and the Nazis the green light for destroying the bookshop but McKeldin, according to the Sun, ordered him to assign police to protect the shop.

A separate police department memo revealed that the Baltimore-Washington AFL-CIO was a top priority target of ISD spying which became particularly intense last spring as Mandel and Pomerleau attempted to break militant strikes in Baltimore by sanitation workers, teachers, and police.

"I don't think you can treat it in isolation. It is part of the nationwide apparatus," Mitchell told the Daily World today. "It definitely ties in with the CIA. We can document that the local ISD sent information to the CIA and the FBI and these these sent information back to ISD.

"I have already written to Church's committee. I told them their investigation of CIA domestic spying will be incomplete unless they look at the role of local police departments as part of the CIA apparatus."

Mitchell said that a request he sent to the Justice Department for an investigation of the ISD plot had been forwarded to the Justice Department's Civil Rights Division.

Rep. Mitchell said he has suspected for years that CIA "dirty tricks" had been used against progressive movements in Baltimore. He recalled a confrontation between Black leaders and Pomerleau in 1971 at the offices of the Baltimore Afro-American, when Pomerleau boasted, "I know when you meet. I know what you plan in your meetings. I know before you meet."

Mitchell added, "Black leaders were spied on, bugged, followed, and reported on until sufficient information was gained to intimidate them into silence and inaction. This was, and is, blackmail as practiced by the police department. It is blatant racism."

Dominic Fornero, president of the Maryland State AFL-CIO, told the *Daily World* today that as the economic crisis worsens and workers fight back, police will lean more heavily on anti-labor spying and provocations.

"I don't think the labor movement is going to take this lying down," Fornero said from his office in Annapolis.

"The people on the picketlines aren't going to take this crap" he said. "It's like the old Gestapo tactics. Pomerleau should be fired. He's got too much of the military in him."

He noted the peculiar silence of Mandel in the face of the scandal. "How can the governor protect a guy like this?" he said. "It seems that Pomerleau gets things on people and then he holds them under his thumb."

Indeed, Baltimore newspapers reported yesterday that the ISD had a stakeout on the governor's mansion in Annapolis. Mandel has been exposed in recent weeks at the center of a growing scandal over kickbacks to some of his top political cronies.

At least three ISD agents were ordered to infiltrate Rep. Mitchell's 1970 election campaign and to photograph Mitchell campaign workers. Mitchell, who is Black, was running at the time against Rep. Sam Friedel, a rabid Vietnam war hawk. On Election Day, dozens of voting machines in Mitchell's strongholds, were mysteriously jammed and Election Board supervisors walked out of the polling places, leaving Baltimore police to count the ballots. Only after a citywide outcry that the election was being stolen did Pomerleau come forward personally and concede that Mitchell had won.

Last month an agent who surfaced was George Guest, one of the agents ordered by Pomerleau to infiltrate Mitchell's campaign and who lifted the lid on the ISD plot.

In hearings before the Maryland State Senate in Annapolis, Guest charged that at least three other spies had been ordered into Mitchell's campaign. "I went to campaign meetings," he said, adding that he reported to the "top echelon ten-officer staff" directly under Pomerleau's command.

Guest accused the Chesapeake & Potomac telephone company of routinely cooperating with the ISD in placing illegal bugs on the telephones of spy victims. His charges were corroborated by other witnesses at the Annapolis hearings.

Thomas Rapanatti, executive director of AFSCME, Police Council 27, revealed a top secret Baltimore Police

Department memo dated Jan. 18, 1974, and signed by Police Lieutenant Peter C. Shaulis of Central Records.

The memo ordered that all "copies of reports" on labor complaints be forwarded to ISD "via the normal distribution system."

George Young, a former Baltimore City policeman, testified that the anti-labor spying in Baltimore is so fanatical that ISD requested information from him on Andrew Lewis, president of the Baltimore-Washington AFL-CIO, after Lewis' death last year.

The ISD memos and testimony by former police officers began to erupt here after Pomerleau and Mandel together viciously smashed the police strike last spring. Hundreds of policemen were demoted or fired after the strike was broken and a flood of memos incriminating Pomerleau began to leak out soon afterwards.

Justice Dept. pushes police arms: UZIS, GAS, To Answer Hungry

By Tim Wheeler

Daily World

WASHINGTON, March 25 (1975)---In its drive to escalate police use of "deadly force" against the people, the U.S. Justice Department helped distribute a 43-page report titled "Submachine Guns in Police Work," it has been learned here.

The report, by David E. Steele, has been mailed to over 700 police departments across the nation. It was prepared late last year at the Police Weapons Center of the International Association of Chiefs of Police (IACP) in Gaithersburg, Md.

The document describes the submachine gun as an "extremely lethal weapon of war" and then explains in exhaustive detail with diagrams, how local police departments can train "special response units" in their use.

Appended to the report are blurbs extolling the virtues of the Israeli "UZI" submachine gun which it says can be purchased from an armaments corporation in

Alexandria, Va. for $120 each, complete with loaded magazine.

An illustrated blurb advertises the MAC M-10 Ingram which fires 1,000 rounds per minute available for $139.50 each from another armaments corporation in Washington.

The report is one of a series commissioned by the Law Enforcement Assistance Administration (LEAA) and kept on file in the LEAA headquarters here where it was examined today by this reporter.

The report disclosed that an informal survey of only 25 police departments unearthed 397 of these automatic weapons stockpiled; one police department alone had an arsenal of 17 such weapons, the report revealed.

"Considering the lack of formal acceptance of submachine guns by the U.S. law enforcement agencies and the almost total absence of training doctrine and policy guidelines for their use, there is a surprising number of these weapons on hand in departments of all sizes in this country," the report states.

The report suggests that submachines might be used to "protect the life of the President" but laments the fact that the "indiscriminate" nature of machine gun fire would endanger the lives of citizens who gather to greet the President.

Machine guns may be useful for guarding government buildings, the report adds.

"The submachine gun," it says, "is most compatible with its designed function in police operations involving raids or assaults on heavily fortified or heavily defended positions. The more closely police operations approximate military combat, the more useful the submachine gun."

It warns that measures must be taken to counteract a strong public reaction against automatic weapons.

"How will the submachine be used?" it asks. "What tactics and general operational guidelines will be employed for managing the submachine gun sub-system?"

Mass indignation, it concludes, can be be neutralized if submachine use is restricted to "carefully selected and trained officers assigned to special response units."

The LEAA is already encouraging formation of these "elite" police units across the nation.

The Los Angeles Police Department has established, at the encouragement of the LEAA a black-shirted unit known as SWAT (Special Weapons and Tactics).

The LEAA gained notoriety recently when it initiated a program of training to combat "food riots."

The authors suggest a model memorandum to be distributed to police departments outlining "policy" on use of automatic weapons including instructions on handling.

"The submachine gun, says the memo, "shall be carried by means of a canvas sling for uniform wear or by means of a sling or holster for concealment under plain clothes."

Credit for the report was taken by the Justice Department in a forward which states, "This document was originally produced by the International Association of Chiefs of Police, for the National Institute of Law Enforcement and Criminal Justice (LEAA), U.S. Department of Justice. The dissemination of his document does not constitute U.S. Department of Justice endorsement or approval of the content."

However, this disclaimer could not conceal the fact that the Justice Department was footing the bill for propaganda in behalf of this menacing escalation of police department firepower across the nation.

Robert Angrosini, press spokesman for the IACP told the *Daily World* today that "research" for the submachine gun report "was funded by the LEAA."

In recent months the LEAA has funded distribution of reports by the Police Weapons Center (PWC) on the "stopping power" of deadly "dum-dum" bullets, the merits of water cannons for breaking up demonstrations, the value of chemical agents such as CS. CN, and DM gas. A special report on "pyrotechnic grenades" including one called the "Federal Speed-heat" describes it as "a time-tested pyrotechnic munition." Another grenade advertised by the PWC is the "Lake Erie Mob Master" grenade.

Reports are devoted to the comparative merits of brands of "nightsticks, blackjacks, saps, special purpose batons, and projectiles."

Also tested in depth were electronic spy gadgets, taps, night-scopes for high-powered rifles and microphones.

A spokesman for the International Armaments Corporation of Alexandria, VA, acknowledged today that his company had "made sales to law enforcement agencies" of "UZI" submachine guns and other automatic weapons.

"All our weapons are strictly imported," said the spokesman, Neil Price, in a telephone interview. "We merely extend a courtesy to law enforcement agencies."

Arrested for Selling Mother's Day Roses
People's Weekly World

May 16, 1984
BALTIMORE—City police swept through downtown Baltimore last Saturday arresting sidewalk vendors who were peddling silk "Mother's Day Roses" without a license—and me for merely asking a question.

Arrested in the Mother's Day eve dragnet were a city worker, father of seven children; an unemployed furniture mover, father of three children; and a young Black woman. I witnessed two of the arrests. When I displayed my press credential and asked one of the arresting officers why the young woman was being arrested, I too was placed under arrest on charges of "failing to obey."

None of the street peddlers were warned in advance that selling notions on the street without a license is illegal. The officers simply walked up to the vendors and demanded they produce their vendor's license. When they could not, the officers, all of whom were white, arrested and handcuffed the vendors, all of whom were Black.

The incident began in downtown Lexington Mall on a breezy, sunny day, the sidewalks crowded with strollers and shoppers. Standing in the middle of the pedestrian mall was Rob, a tall young Afro-American man urging people to buy his merchandise. Then I observed a cop handcuffing the young seller of silk roses.

I turned and walked toward Howard Street. A large crowd had gathered around a squad car parked in the middle of the mall. I made my way through the crowd. A police officer was just then twisting the arms of a young Black woman behind her back and clamping handcuffs on her wrists. Two boxes of the roses were strewn at her feet. Tears were streaming down her cheeks. She pleaded, "I've never been in trouble before. I didn't know it was against the law. Please let me go." The grim-faced cop finished handcuffing her and began speaking into his shoulder radio.

I held out my press credential and called out to the officer, "Why are you arresting her?"

A second officer standing at the rear of the squad car fixed me with a menacing stare and shouted, "Move." I displayed my credential and repeated my question. Again, the officer ordered me to "move." Then I asked the officer if the woman had been warned. "You are under arrest," the second officer said, spinning me against the squad car and clamping handcuffs on my wrists.

A few seconds later, the young Black man was brought back and pushed into the back of the squad car beside me along with our arresting officer. We were transported at breakneck speed to the distant Southwest District Police Station. The young woman was taken to the Central Station in downtown Baltimore. I have been unable, so far, to discover her fate.

I was stripped of all my possessions—my wallet, pens papers, notebooks, belt, and shoelaces—and booked. I was fingerprinted. I telephoned my lawyer and was then locked in cell Number 9.

The rose peddler, who introduced himself to me as "Rob," was in cell Number 6, diagonally across the corridor.

The inmate in cell Number 8, arrested that morning for interstate flight to avoid prosecution for possession of stolen property—a car—and marijuana and cocaine, announced to us that he was a "three-time loser." Then he asked: "What was you guys busted for?"

Replied Rob, "Selling roses."

"Selling what?" asked inmate Number 8, disbelief in his voice.

"Selling Mother's Day roses," Rob repeated.

Laughter echoed in the cell block.

Directly across from me in cell Number 4 was Al, a city employee, father of seven, who spoke freely to me about his situation but asked that I not use his full name. "If the city finds out I was busted, I could lose my job," he said.

Al was arrested an hour or so earlier in the same drag-net, for selling Mother's Day roses without a license. "I just can't feed my wife and seven kids on the pay I get from my city job," he said. "I peddle notions on the week-ends to help pay rent. The police harass us constantly. If we stay away from the downtown, we can usually avoid being arrested. But I figure that's where the people would be the day before Mother's Day. I was just trying to make an honest dollar," he said, "just trying to make it through hard times."

Rob said he had been laid off eight months from his job as a furniture mover and hauler and is supporting his wife and three children on whatever he can earn sell-ing trinkets, belts, and artificial flowers on the street.

The peddlers, he said, pick up the merchandise from several wholesale warehouses in downtown Baltimore.

He said he paid twenty-four dollars for two boxes of silk roses and had sold thirty dollars' worth by the time he was arrested. He also had another nine dollars in extra cash in his pocket for a total of thirty-nine dollars at the time of his arrest. "Just my luck they'll set bail at $500. I'll need forty dollars for the bail bondsman. I'll be one dollar short," Rob said ruefully.

A third peddler, Steve, also arrested that morning, sat silently on the oak bench in his cell holding his head in his hands—in obvious despair. "I've got a part-time job as a dishwasher at a downtown restaurant," he said. "I'm supposed to be at work at six o'clock. They'll probably fire me. I've got a wife and two kids and another on the way."

Steve said he knows eighty or more street peddlers personally. "Most of them got laid off at Sparrows Point (Bethlehem Steel) or from some other job," he said. "My brother-in-law was earning eleven dollars an hour at Western Electric before they shut it down. Now he's on the street, a family to support. The only thing left is peddling."

I asked him how his wife will take his arrest. "Hard," he replied. "She'll take it hard." He paused for a long moment. "I'd do almost anything to get a full-time job," he said. "Any job. Anything to be able to support myself and my family."

Rob stood with his forearms resting on the steel cross bars, also staring out into the corridor. We were all waiting. "All this for selling roses," he said with a deep sigh. "It makes you want to give up."

Epilogue: My lawyer is Harold Buchman, the best civil liberties lawyer in Baltimore. A few minutes before my trial was to begin, he met with the state's attorney who agreed not to press charges in exchange for my promise not to initiate action against the arresting officer.

Street peddler Al was also let off, perhaps because he has a job and is supporting seven children.

Unrepresented by an attorney, Rob stood ramrod straight as the judge set his fine at $150. "Do you have the money on you?" asked the judge. "No, your honor," replied Rob. "Put this man in jail," snapped the judge. At $10 per day, it will be fifteen days before Rob is a free man.

Voters Sign for Hall, Davis in Charm City
Daily World

August 21, 1984
BALTIMORE---As I was gathering signatures for Gus Hall and Angela Davis on an East Baltimore street the

other day, a young woman stopped me in mid-sentence. "They aren't Republicans are they?" she demanded. "No, they're Communists," I replied. "Fine," she replied, and signed.

Her statement was not any more hostile to the administration of Ronald Reagan than several thousand other angry comments I heard from signers of our petitions during the last eight weeks. The rage against Reagan's "steal-from-the-poor, give-to-the-rich" economic game plan is palpable.

But what stopped me short was the implication of her question that she would not sign the petition if it had been seeking ballot status for Reagan. Yet she gladly signed to place the candidates of the Communist Party USA on the ballot.

The Reagan-Bush campaign would be hard pressed if they had to collect 10,000 signatures on the street to get their candidates on the ballot in Baltimore. This may be a more reliable referendum on voters' attitudes towards Reagan than the so-called "scientific" polls of Gallup and Harris. The very mention of Reagan's name prompted expressions of disgust from the overwhelming majority of voters I spoke to.

On the other hand, these same voters expressed strong support for the anti-big business, pro-peace specifics of the Hall-Davis platform. Especially among young Afro-American women, I found a powerful identification with Angela Davis. East Baltimore steelworkers know who Gus Hall is and most wanted him on the ballot.

We've come a long way since the depths of McCarthyism. No one on the streets petitioning today can fail to be impressed by the mood of fearlessness among the people. Reagan has flopped in his attempts to incite witch-hunt anti-Communism.

Working street corners for eight weeks proved that the run-down, inner city sections of Baltimore are not Baltimore's "mean streets;" they are the "kindly streets." The "mean streets" are in Guilford and Homewood with their fake Georgian mansions, English gardens, Mercedes Benz' and strange air of being uninhabited.

On East Monument Street we developed kindred feelings for street vendors, most of whom signed our petitions. Seven or eight hours on the street each day gathering seventy-five or more signatures for Hall and Davis gave a new meaning to the word "hustle."

Signature gathering is a bit like prospecting for gold and some neighborhoods of Baltimore, East Monument Street, for example, was a seemingly inexhaustible lode. The street was paved with signatures. Citywide, one in every three or four persons we approached signed. On East Monument Street seven or eight out of ten persons we approached signed. One petitioner gathered as many as 200 signatures a day there using two clipboards. It is a mostly Black but still significantly integrated shopping area a couple of blocks east of John Hopkins Hospital. The shoppers included hundreds of hospital workers who signed in droves.

Why should the response there have been so much warmer than, say, Lexington Mall, the main downtown shopping center, where we also collected seven thousand or so signatures? Could one factor be our distribution over the past decade of tens of thousands of *Daily Worlds* in the solidly working class neighborhoods adjacent to that East Monument Street shopping area? There is a time to sow and a time to reap.

If our attitude towards Baltimore changed, so did the attitude of the Baltimoreans towards us. After five weeks on the streets, we became a more or less permanent fixture. True, some became a bit impatient at being asked repeatedly to sign our petitions. "I already signed at the unemployment office . . . Gay Street . . . Lexington Mall . . . Waverly," people would exclaim.

We shared the street with petitioners from other campaigns. The most bizarre I encountered was a woman in high heels and heavy make-up who sidled up to me on Lexington Mall one day. With a sigh, she reported that she had been on the streets all day and had yet to collect a single signature.

Furtively, as if displaying an obscene postcard, she peeled back a corner of the folder she held tightly against her chest. Concealed inside was a petition from the Reagan-Bush campaign with a red, white, and blue headline. "Thank you, President Reagan!!!!" Like a Marine patrolling downtown Beirut, she retreated up the Mall and vanished. We never saw that petition again.

We had hundreds of people coming up to us asking, "How is it going? Are you going to make it?" I even had a few who asked "Are WE going to make it?"

A proprietary claim on this city began to awaken in us. And petition signers, in turn, began to view Hall and Davis' campaign as their own. I think they were also attracted by the element of dramatic suspense. Here was this stubborn band of men and women, defying Reaganite redbaiting, on the street every day and racing the deadline to get the required 10,000 signatures.

There may not be dancing in the streets. But in the homes of several thousand workingclass families in Baltimore, a silent cheer is going up if and when we win ballot status. The victory will belong to those 16,515 men and women who signed our petitions.

(We did win a place on the ballot, collecting over 20,000 signatures, and also a place on the ballot in Washington, D.C. where we worked alternate weekends. We owe winning a ballot place in D.C. to a ruling by an African American judge who ordered the D.C. Election Commissioner to honor the many thousands of signatures we collected in our nation's capital. But the vote for the Hall-Davis ticket was disappointingly small in both cities. It showed that for a majority of signers, their motivation was upholding our democratic right to be on the ballot. They were also supporting our right to present our platform on basic issues. They wanted voters to have choices other than Republican and Democrat).

Handing Out the News to the 99%
People's World

NEW YORK---Alberta Friscia, a staff writer and photographer for the *Daily World* snapped a photo of me long ago striking a jaunty pose with a bundle of *Daily Worlds* balanced on top of my head.

She must have taken the photo at a big peace or labor rally because I am wearing a *Daily World* apron. That

suggests I was not armed with a notepad and ballpoint pen covering the event but rather joining with the *DW* team in distributing the paper to the crowd.

The photo brought back happy recollections of my adventures handing out many thousands of our paper at plant gates such as the Bethlehem Steel Sparrows Point mill or door-to-door in East Baltimore or at huge demonstrations on the Capitol Mall in Washington D.C. Those newspapers often carried headline articles I had written. As I handed the paper to a peace marcher, I would say: "Check out that front page article. I wrote it."

I admit, vanity was a factor in my enthusiasm for distributing the paper.

At these events, I joined teams of twenty or thirty or even 100 comrades who fanned out with bundles of papers saturating the crowd with our paper.

Yet on other occasions, I was the lone distributor. Sometime in the mid-1970s, the AFL-CIO Building and Construction Trades Department met at a hotel in Washington D.C. I was assigned to cover it and had my

AFL-CIO credential dangling from my neck. But the *DW* also sent down bundles of the paper to be distributed to the 1,000 or more delegates.

It should have been a task for the Washington D.C. Club of the Communist Party but none of the comrades could make it. So the task fell to me.

I went to the Greyhound Depot early one morning and picked up the bundles, drove to the Sheraton Hotel. I parked the car and lugged the bundles into the hotel. I found a corridor with a heavy flow of union delegates and started handing them out as fast as I could move my hand. The delegates were grabbing them, their faces buried in the front page reading as they hurried off to a plenary session.

Of course, I had to cover that session so I was in a hurry to hand the paper out but also delighted by the eagerness of these trade unionists in accepting the paper.

Then out of nowhere, a very large Sergeant-at-Arms appeared. "What are you doing?" he snapped.

"I'm distributing the *Daily World.*"

"Who authorized this?"

"No one. I didn't know I needed authorization."

"Well, you do. Leave immediately or I'll have you arrested."

"I believe in freedom of the press and I plan to stay."

"I'm going for backup. If you are still here when I return, you will be arrested."

He rushed off down the corridor. I was in a terrible sweat. Not only would I be left with papers undistributed, I would lose my credential and not be able to cover the afternoon session when Senator Ted Kennedy was scheduled to deliver one of his stemwinders.

Yet, as the sweat trickled from my brow, I was still handing out the paper as quickly as I could. I worked for just a couple of minutes longer and then looked down the hall and saw the Sergeant-at-Arms looming in the distance with two other beefy enforcers bearing down on me. I bent, picked up the bundle of papers, preparing to turn and run.

Then suddenly a cheery voice rang out. "Tim! Tim Wheeler. It's so good to see you!"

I turned, and who should I see hurrying down the hall from the opposite direction but Lou Weinstock, a revered leader of the Painters Union and also a member of the National Committee of the Communist Party USA. Lou was bubbling with as much enthusiasm as he was that day in the 1930s when he leaped from a balcony onto a chandelier in the ballroom of a Cincinnati hotel during a convention of the AFL. He shouted at the delegates that long ago day to "Stop Starvation NOW" by joining the struggle to win Unemployment Compensation.

"Tim, I'm so glad you are here," Lou exclaimed. "I want you to meet my friend. He's the International President of the Painters Union." And sure enough, there right beside him was S. Frank "Bud" Raftery, President of the International Union of Painters & Allied Trades. Raftery was a staunch progressive beloved by union painters and other building trades workers everywhere. He was a close friend of Lou Weinstock.

Raftery shook my hand warmly. Lou took two copies of the *DW* from me and handed one of them to Raftery. "Here Bud, here's something for you to read during the next coffee break."

I glanced over my shoulder in time to see the Sergeant-at-Arms come to a screeching halt. He and his fellow security agents, looking like NFL lineman, beat a hasty retreat back up the corridor.

As Lou and Raftery strolled off down the hall, I completed the distribution of the paper. I still had ample time to get back to the ballroom in time to hear Kennedy rip the greedy corporate elite.

Not all these adventures took place in Washington, D.C. In the late 1980s, I was sent down to New Orleans to cover a national "Black Power Summit" at one of the largest convention hotels. About 2,000 delegates from all over the U.S. came to this gathering. It included twelve leaders of the CPUSA led by Jim Jackson and Charlene Mitchell. The Party contingent met in a hotel room to strategize. At the end of the meeting, the question of distributing the 800 copies of the *DW* that had been sent down on the Greyhound bus was discussed. We went around the room and everyone had an assignment that made it impossible for them to help distribute the paper. Again, it fell to me.

We must have had a rental car. I can't remember. Somehow, I drove to the Greyhound Depot, picked up the eight bundles of papers and returned to the hotel. I unloaded them on the sidewalk right in front of the hotel and went to park the car. When I got back, I opened a bundle and started to hand them out.

Inside, a plenary session was coming to an end. It was evening and the delegates were headed to Louis Armstrong Park for a night of jazz and celebration. They began to stream out and I was handing the paper to them as fast as I could move my hand.

The hotel doorman, a tall, powerfully built African American man dressed in pearl gray livery with a top hat caught sight of me and approached. "What are you doing, sir?" he demanded. Again, I quelled the urge to drop the papers, turn and run.

"Well," I said. "I'm trying to distribute this paper."

He glanced down at the bundles of *DW*s behind me. "You's got a whole lot of papers to distribute by yourself. Let me give you a hand."

With that, he removed his white gloves, stooped, picked up a bundle of papers and began handing them to the delegates as they boarded the chartered buses. Soon, his hands were moving as fast as mine.

Somehow, we managed to distribute every copy of the paper. I stepped over to where he was standing and shook his hand. "It went well," he told me. "The delegates were happy to receive your paper." He flashed a genial smile. "I better go in and wash my hands. They're covered with ink."

There is a reason New Orleans is nicknamed "The Big Easy." It's not just the Mississippi that flows by the town. I will not soon forget that hotel doorman who came to my rescue that day.

I could go on about the joy I got over the years in handing out a movement paper bringing news the people rarely get in the commercial for-profit media, "News for the 99%." When we joined the Great Peace March for Nuclear Disarmament in Indiana in 1986, we wrote about the progress of the march heading for Washington D.C. We filed a story every day. The office in New York printed it and bundles were shipped back to distribute to the marchers. I joined the march in Youngstown and marched to Pittsburgh writing a story every day and helping local comrades distribute the bundle when it was delivered. In Pittsburgh, someone else took my place, as I recall, Marilyn Bechtel.

When the Pittston Coal Miners went on strike, our correspondents covered it. Denise Winebrenner and Scott Marshall were invited by the miners to join in their courageous occupation of a Pittston Mine Portal in Southwest Virginia reminiscent of the Flint Sitdown in the 1930s. Again, we shipped bundles down and distributed them to the coal miners.

In 1996, the United Steelworkers went on strike against Wheeling-Pitt. The strike would last over a year, the longest work stoppage in steel industry history. Again my paper, by now named the *People's Weekly World* (*PWW*), covered that strike extensively and in depth. I was the editor of the *PWW* and traveled to Youngstown and to Follansbee, West Virginia to cover the strike—and also to distribute the *PWW*.

When a comrade, a Pittsburgh woman schoolteacher, and I arrived in Follansbee, the town, a majority Italian-American, were preparing to celebrate Garibaldi Day. The highlight was a parade and already thousands of citizens had set up folding chairs along main street and were sitting waiting for the parade to begin.

I dropped the comrade at the far end of the street with a couple of bundles of the *PWW*. Then I drove to the other end. We worked our way toward each other passing out the paper to every resident waiting for the parade to begin.

When we finished, we looked back up main street. Virtually everyone in town was reading the paper!

I even remember the banner headline that blazed from that edition over the front page article written by Denise Winebrenner: "We Are Union in This Valley." It is the best headline I have ever seen on any newspaper.

In my half century as a staff writer and editor, we probably distributed well over a million copies of our twenty page paper. Some of those who accepted the paper paid the 50¢ cover price. I remember Frank Soifer. Frank joked that he was chosen for his august position as chairperson of the Communist Party of Oregon "by a process of elimination." Soifer raised over $1,000 annually by selling the paper to the residents of Eugene where he lived. Frank's tactic when he handed the paper to a passersby was to say, "free...donations accepted." Hundreds of people would give him a dollar and say, "Keep the change."

Yet these donations did not begin to cover the cost of the hundreds of thousands of papers we distributed. How did we cover those costs? Fundraising! Every year we raised $200,000 or more to keep the paper afloat. We organized banquets, potluck suppers, flea markets, garage sales, bake sales, and mass meetings featuring guest speakers. We celebrated when these events brought in anywhere from $500 to $5,000.

Once I gained a reputation as an enjoyable speaker to listen to, I was sent out on speaking tours to help raise money to sustain the paper. In 1991, I spoke in twenty-four cities and towns, at events that brought in more than $40,000. After speaking at a kickoff rally in New York City, I spoke at Cleveland State University. But when I returned to Rick Nagin's home after that speech, I could not find my airline ticket. Rick and I were on the phone to officials at Cleveland State. I even think Rick drove back to the campus and searched the auditorium where I spoke. I had been scheduled to return home to Baltimore before resuming the tour. I paid for a ticket to fly home, eaten up with anxiety over the missing ticket.

I was getting ready to buy a replacement when the phone rang. A janitor had found my ticket under the seats in the front row of the auditorium where I had been sitting before I spoke. It had been in the inside pocket of the sport coat I was wearing and somehow fell on the floor. It would have cost me a couple thousand dollars to replace that ticket. Someone in the central office of Cleveland State overnighted it to me. It arrived just in time. The rest of the tour was, in my personal opinion, a triumph!

The *People's World*, today, is environmentally friendly and no longer publishes on newsprint. Yet we know that this online publication is read by hundreds of thousands of readers on their laptops or desk computers or at the local library. The cyber revolution has opened the way for us to reach millions.

Yet I draw some lessons from my years of distributing our paper, feeling the personal warmth of meeting people face-to-face to talk with them about the most burning issues of the day. We no longer need to haul those bundles to the next demonstration or strike picketline. We no longer struggle every year to raise the money to pay for them.

But we still need to get out and talk to people face-to-face, to convince them that we all need to join the movement to defend democracy and fight for the progressive change we all know is necessary. And yes, we also need to do lots of fundraising to pay for it. News for the 99% is not free.

We've Got Friends Everywhere
People's Daily World

February 1991
LOS ANGELES—Last Sunday was Sadie Doroshkin's ninetieth birthday and a big crowd of Angelenos turned out to celebrate her tireless work for the *People's Weekly World* and its predecessors. Folk singer Jerry Atinsky sang her a birthday song. Tony Saidy, former president of the

L.A. chapter of the American Arab Anti-Discrimination Committee spoke and so did I. The crowd contributed $4,500 in cash and $6,500 in pledges. The *World's* Los Angeles reporter, Rosalio Muñoz, told me it was an excellent start on Southern California's $60,000 goal.

In San Francisco Friday night, I shared the platform with Fuad Mansour, president of the Bay Area Palestine Aid Society. But the show-stoppers were Farcia DeTolles and Anzania Howse, two young African-American women in the U.S. Army Reserve who refused orders to the Persian Gulf. They are fighting to win CO status.

They blasted the genocidal bombing of Iraqi men, women and children. "Our fight is here at home against the racist policies of President George Bush," they said. The crowd answered with a standing ovation. Over $7,000 was collected for the paper.

It has been this way in nearly all the thirteen cities I have spoken in so far. Peace and justice activists speak at these *PWW* events, or help fill the seats to hear our interpretation of Bush's "hidden agenda" in the Gulf war. They are young and old, with many Arab-Americans in attendance as well as African-Americans and Latinos. Every event has been followed by a question and answer period.

Although the shooting and bombing are over, interest is not slacking. In Salt Lake City, I spoke at the University of Utah. One man told the audience he graduated from West Point in the same class as National Security Adviser Brent Snowcroft. "I know him well. He was a schemer then and he's a schemer now," he said.

In Portland, Oregon, my sister, Susan Elizabeth, my brother Steve and his wife Carlyn and *PWW* readers organized a potluck dinner. The house was packed and the food was sumptuous. More than $900 was collected with the help of Hank and Martina Curl who handed in a check for $500. They distribute 400 papers at the gates of the Swann Island shipyard. "Since the Gulf War, the workers just grab the paper," said Martina. "They are really hungry for some real news about the war."

The Mother Who Said, "Nyet, Nyet!"
By Tim Wheeler
People's Weekly World

Based on s story in the Daily World in Sept. 1980.
BALTIMORE---My daughter, Susan Melissa Wheeler, was
a wee lass of twelve when she made her first trip to the
Soviet Union in the summer of 1980. She was recruited
by Rachel Rubin, only a few years her senior, who would
serve as the guide of this expedition. Rachel also recruited
Jennifer Kramer, even younger than Susan.

It was her grandmother, Leatha Provost, who provided the money to pay the airfare, meals, and lodging
for Susan's trip. Of course, Joyce and I were filled with
grave doubts about allowing our darling child to under-
take such a long journey to a land so foreign you could
not even read the alphabet unless you could decipher
Cyrillic. It was also a land that had been demonized for
decades by Cold Warriors who whipped up a climate of
fear for everything going on behind the "Iron Curtain."

But Rachel was mature beyond her years and we
were soon reassured that Susan was in safe hands and
headed for a country that would provide for her safety.

If we had known what would befall Susan on her journey, we probably would have nixed the entire project.
Soon after they arrived at their hotel in Moscow and
converted a few dollars to rubles and kopecks, Rachel
suggested they hike down to Red Square, a half hour
walk away. Susan and Jennifer thought it was a splendid idea even though Susan was feeling the effects of
jet-lag and wanted above all else to stretch out and sleep.

They emerged onto the street and strolled along staring
at all the strange and fascinating sights of the great city.
The weather was perfect, the sun shining, the streets
crowded with Muscovites hurrying along.

They trudged down Gorki Street for many blocks.
Suddenly the avenue opened up into a vast cobblestone
plaza with the crenulated brick walls of the Kremlin in
the distance, the towers topped with spires and glowing

red stars at their peak. There was the mausoleum of V.I. Lenin and in the distance the whimsical, multi-colored St. Basil's Cathedral. Susan, Rachel and Jennifer were awestruck by this spectacle. They walked down toward Lenin's mausoleum and joined a vast crowd of tourists watching the changing of the guard. Ramrod stiff Red Army soldiers holding their rifles straight up at arm's length, goose-stepped their way through a complicated ritual.

Yet all the excitement, the heat of the day suddenly hit Susan. She was overcome with exhaustion, feeling dizzy. "I'm not feeling very well, Rachel. I think I will head back to the hotel. You and Jennifer can stay here. I can make it by myself."

Rachel agreed.

So Susan departed, walking back across Red Square. She came to a bus stop that looked like it traveled along the route they had walked. She boarded the bus and dropped the kopeck in the fare box. The bus trundled along from stop to stop. It was packed with passengers so it was difficult for her to keep an eye on where the bus was going. It entered a circle and turned off on a radial spoke. She no longer recognized the buildings as they flashed by.

When the bus stopped, she stepped off onto the side-walk. Across a public square was a Metro Station with throngs of men and women hustling down the escalator into the subway tunnel or up from underground and stepping out onto the sidewalk in a steady stream. She stood for several minutes, feeling the heartbeat of this huge city, teeming with people, all of them seemingly in a hurry.

She turned around. Nothing was familiar to her. She did not recognize where she had come from. The street signs were in that unreadable Cyrillic alphabet.

"Where am I? How can I find my way back?"

Panic engulfed her. She kept turning around, staring at the buildings, the streets, hoping to see something she recognized. The crowd swept around her, hurrying in every direction, often chatting loudly in a language she did not understand.

Then she stood stock still, trembling with fear, overcome by the hopelessness of her situation. Tears welled in her eyes and streamed down her cheeks.

It seemed an eternity she stood weeping.

Then out of the crowd came a woman, gripping the hand of her own daughter. She spoke to the child beside her, then dropped the little girl's hand and took Susan by the arm, asking questions Susan did not understand and could not answer.

The tears were flowing freely now and the mother cradled Susan's cheeks in her hands. With her thumbs she wiped away the tears from Susan's cheeks. "Nyet, nyet," she said.

Then the woman resumed her questions. Susan's Russian vocabulary consisted of "Da" "Nyet" "Spliseba" and "Dos vedanya." They stood like this trying to communicate for minutes.

Then Susan had a brainstorm.

"My hotel key!" she said out loud. She fished in her jacket pocket and pulled out the key with the plastic tag identifying the hotel where Susan, Rachel and Jennifer were staying.

"Da!" the mother exclaimed, taking the key to examine it. She gave Susan a bear hug, took her own daughters hand in one hand and Susan's in the other and walked to the curb. She hailed a cab and got everyone in. She gave the driver instructions. Off the cab sped. The hotel, it turned out was only a few blocks away.

"Oh, there it is! If only I had known. It was so near!" Susan said to her uncomprehending fellow travelers.

The cab came to a halt. They all piled out on the sidewalk. The mother spoke to the hotel doorman. Susan opened her purse and pulled out a five ruble note.

"Nyet, nyet," the mother said, giving Susan one last hug before she climbed back into the cab with her daughter. Susan did not even know the woman's name.

She went into the hotel—now she knew it was named "The Eagle Hotel" and made her way to her room and fell exhausted onto her bed. She was fast asleep when she heard a key in the door lock and Rachel and Jennifer returned.

Decades later we still recall that moment in Susan's life. It was not such a surprising thing for a mother to do, seeing a girl who could have been her own daughter lost in a far off land. I think of that lovely line about Ruth in John Keats' poem, Ode to a Nightingale: "Sick for home, she stood in tears amid the alien corn."

I like to think that if that mother's daughter had been lost on a street corner in Baltimore, a mother would step forward and rescue her, wipe away her tears, embrace her, take her by the hand and lead her part way home.

A Chance to beat Reaganomics
Daily World

March 1983

CHICAGO---Chicago's African American mayoral candidate, Harold Washington, had a blunt warning for the Democratic Committee of Cook County when he spoke to a labor breakfast at the Conrad Hilton, here, recently.

Washington, who won the Democratic primary in a three-way race February 22, told the cheering crowd of Afro-American and white trade unionists that he expects the Cook County Democratic Party of its own "volition" to support him in his race against Republican Bernard Epton, concluding in the April 12 general election.

Washington praised his backers, the independent, grassroots movement which had whipped Chicago's reactionary "Daley machine" in the primary. He warned Fast Eddie

Vrdolyak, the Democratic machine boss, that he would not "slink through the streets like a thief to beg for their endorsement."

If the Democrats refuse to endorse and actively support his campaign, he said, it will mean the "death knell" of the Democrats. If they refuse, he added, "I will with gusto, alacrity, and firmness preside over the demise of the Democratic Party."

These were strong words, backed by a powerful people's movement! And the crowd, about one third of whom were white trade unionists, roared its agreement.

Yet the corporate-financial elite that rules Chicago is so terrified by this movement that they have, as one resident put it to me, "gone berserk." And it is not just the local ruling class that fears the movement that has selected Washington as its standard bearer. Senator Paul Laxalt, chairman of the National Republican Party, President Reagan's best friend, and other GOP big wigs have attempted to dump Bernard Epton and convince the discredited incumbent Mayor Jane Byrne, a lifelong Democrat, to run as a Republican. However, Epton has refused to cooperate by stepping down and Byrne will run a write-in campaign.

Reagan's crude attempt at a "bi-partisan" racist maneuver against Washington is dictated by the Afro-American congressman's practice of treating Reagan as the real "enemy" in his campaign. In virtually every speech, Washington zeroes in on Reagan's steal-from-the-poor, give-to-the-rich policies as the main source of the nation's urban crisis. In his labor breakfast speech, Washington vowed to "bury" Reaganism April 12.

Washington is continuing to solidify his base among Afro-American voters who displayed their muscle February 22. But Washington is now conspicuously running to be the mayor of all the people of Chicago. His watchword is "heal." And by that word he refers to the wounds inflicted on Afro-American, Puerto Rican, Mexican-American, and white people by decades of Daleyite racism. He is asking for—and he needs—a huge vote from Chicago's white voters.

Washington is telling us that he recognizes that a close, racially polarized vote will encourage the machine to continue a policy of massive resistance even if he is elected. A big, decisive victory, on the other hand, would inflict a sharp, if not lethal blow on the machine.

This presents Chicago's labor movement, its progressive religious and community organizations with the biggest opportunity—and its biggest challenge—in history. All notions of "writing off" vast sections of the white population, characterizing them as "racist," must be combatted. Ways can and must be· found to broaden the already emerging Afro-American-white unity in the Washington campaign. These white masses can be reached through their unions, churches, synagogues, and community groups..

Washington, himself, is providing the opening. By identifying Reagan and Reaganism as his opponent, he is helping white masses to see that they and Chicago's Afro-American community share a common enemy who can only be defeated by interracial unity. Millions of white Chicagoans, suffering the joblessness and misery of "Reaganomics" can be convinced to join this independent voter movement. They can be persuaded to vote for Washington.

But for that to happen, white progressives active in Washington's campaign will have to overcome some deep-seated anti-working class hang-ups and carry the campaign into the white wards.

As several observers stated while this reporter was covering Washington's' campaign recently, "the eyes of the nation are on Chicago." A big, decisive, victory for Washington will be a "prelude to 1984" and the Presidential and Congressional elections that could smash Reaganism beyond repair.

Chapter 6

Florida: Hurricanes, Lynchings, A Very American Coup

It didn't take us long to decide we needed to fly a reporter down to West Palm Beach, Florida in the first week of November 2000.

All hell had broken lose as voters, enraged by the confusing "butterfly ballot," descended on the Palm Beach County Board of Elections in big crowds chanting, "Count Every Vote" and "Re-Vote, Re-Vote!"

They were especially angry that the ballot was so confusing that many people of Jewish background ended up mistakenly casting their ballots for Republican Patrick Buchanan, a raving anti-Semite.

I got the assignment and flew immediately to Florida where I was met at the airport by Sid Taylor, organizer of the Florida Communist Party, Lou Kalb, a Party stalwart and other members of the West Palm Beach CP club.

That same day we drove down to the Board of Elections where a thousand or more demonstrators were protesting.

It was obvious that the Republican Party was orchestrating a full-fledged drive to stop the vote count and steal the 2000 election for George W. Bush.

I was to be on assignment in Florida for several weeks on that trip, covering the mass demonstrations across the Sunshine State as election board staff toiled to recount the ballots with their dangling chads. I offer here a few of the articles I wrote during that struggle.

Yet it was not the first time I had been assigned to Florida. *Daily World* Managing Editor, Si Gerson, and I covered both the Republican and Democratic Conventions in Miami Beach in 1972. I wrote stories about the mass demonstrations that converged on the GOP convention, the brutal beatings by the police, the clouds of tear gas, the mass arrests.

We stayed at one of those lovely art deco hotels in South Miami Beach. We visited Abe and Ruth (their last name escapes me right now), working class retirees who lived in South Miami Beach. Abe operated a Marxist news stand right on a street corner in Miami Beach where the *Daily World* was sold. Both were active in the Jewish Cultural Center, which had a magnificent large meeting hall at the far south end of town. During the GOP convention, an anti-war rally was convened at the Jewish Cultural Center featuring actress Jane Fonda, who had just returned from Vietnam.

Ruth, a tiny, spritely woman, a fiery stump speaker, introduced Fonda as a hero of the anti-war movement. I was sitting right beside Fonda and heard her giggling with delight at Ruth's generous introduction. I don't remember the particulars of Fonda's speech, but it was about the atrocities inflicted on the people by Nixon's carpet bombing of Vietnam. I didn't disagree. Jane Fonda was a hero of the anti-war movement.

In the years that followed, I was myself a guest speaker at the Jewish Cultural Center, then chaired by a wonderful comrade Vito Magli. The organization had been forced to sell their center and move to a far smaller space.

I also traveled to Florida to cover the devastation inflicted by several hurricanes. It is amazing to me that every disaster, natural or man-made, has a political dimension. Disasters expose to the light of day the difference between villains and heroes, between people who care nothing for human suffering, and the decent people who throw themselves into the struggle to rescue and rebuild.

On a trip to Tampa, I wrote a story about the frame-up of Dr. Sami Al Arian, a computer science professor at South Florida University, and the fightback waged by his courageous wife Nahla.

I also include in this chapter, my article, *The Sacrifice of Harry & Harriette Moore*, murdered by the KKK as they slept in their modest bungalow in Mims, Florida, Christmas night, 1951.

That centerspread article appeared February 24, 2001, just before I flew on a trip to West Palm Beach. When I got off the plane, Sid Taylor embraced me.

"Oh my God, what a magnificent article you have written about Harry & Harriette Moore," he said. "It brought tears to my eyes. It is going to help us in our work here in Florida. We are going to reprint it and get it out widely." I offer in the pages that follow a few of the stories I wrote about Florida.

1,100 Arrested as Nixon Talks 'Peace'
Daily World

August 25, 1972
MIAMI BEACH, Florida; August 24—President Nixon shielded himself from the people last night with a ring of steel, club-wielding Florida troopers and clouds of tear gas as he talked "peace" in his re-nomination acceptance speech. Rampaging troopers arrested 1,100, including 840 men and 170 women.

Inside the convention, four Vietnam Veterans Against the War, three in wheelchairs, voiced their dissent from the Nixon war policies, in a demonstration ignored by the TV cameras. They had been admitted into the hall in a GOP public relations gesture to the war wounded. One of the four was William Wyman, double amputee from Placitas, New Mexico.

As Wyman wheeled himself in his aluminum chair hurriedly down the corridor of the Convention Hall, he told the *Daily World*, "I came here to talk to the people. I want to tell them how Nixon lied to the people, how he ran on a peace platform four years ago but didn't keep his word."

The others were Bob Mullen, of Great Neck, Long Island; Ron Kovac of Los Angeles; and De Mark Clevenger, hometown not given.

During Nixon's speech they shouted, "Stop the Bombing," and held up a sign with that demand. They were hustled from the hall by FBI security agents.

500 still in jail

At nine-thirty this morning, 500 of those arrested were still incarcerated at the Dade County Jail, the county stockade, bringing to 1,300 the total arrests during this Republican convention, called a "family reunion" by the GOP top command.

An estimated sixty were injured last night with head lacerations, including a Miami news reporter whose head was cracked open by a trooper as he stood on the sidewalk. Six stitches were required to close the wound on his forehead. A Black Miami channel 7 TV newsman was clubbed and his photographer's camera was smashed.

Bus-encircled fortress

Convention Hall was a fortress yesterday, encircled with Miami city buses parked bumper to bumper, as squadrons of brown-shirted Florida highway troopers flew at the youthful demonstrators, clubbing them with cold fury.

Tear gas grenades popped like firecrackers along Collins Avenue. Youths and residents of Miami Beach were hit by the eye-stinging pepper gas which engulfed the downtown and the surrounding residential areas.

Delegates scurried to the shelter of the Convention Hall, handkerchiefs to their noses. Helicopters wheeled overhead. The canals that crisscross Miami Beach, used as moats, were patrolled by the Coast Guard and the Marine Patrol.

The police attack opened late yesterday as demonstrators marched from Flamingo Park toward the Doral

Hotel, the Miami Beach headquarters of the White House, and also Convention headquarters.

The Miami Coalition, an organization of all the anti-war groups here, has planned to present to the White House the "findings" of a two-day investigation of Nixon's crimes against the poor of Indochina and the U.S.

500 reach hotel

A march of 500 to the Doral headed by peace activist David Dellinger and Father James Groppi succeeded finally in reaching its goal late last night after the orgy of arrests and tear-gassing by Miami police had subsided.

However, Dellinger, Groppi and about 200 other participants were arrested when they sat down in the street in front of the lush, closely guarded "no public allowed" hotel.

This correspondent and *Daily World* editor S. W. Gerson were among the newsmen teargassed in the initial assault on the demonstrators at about 6 p.m. last night at 34th and Collins Avenue.

The anti-war youths were obviously divided, with the Miami Coalition groups and Vietnam Veterans Against the War participating in the mass non-violent sit-down protests while incidents of "trashing" were instigated by anarchist groups such as the Zippies and Students for a Democratic Society. It was these later isolated incidents that the police used as a pretext for their attack.

"What do you think you're doing?" a veteran shouted to the Zippies as he attempted to halt the trashing. "What effect do you think this is going to have?"

Packed in airtight vans

The police used rent-a-truck vans, virtually airtight and totally dark inside, to transport hundreds of arrested demonstrators to jail. The demonstrators, many of them with head wounds and choking from tear gas, were hurled into the vans and the airtight doors were slammed shut.

Escorted by motorcycle police, their sirens screaming, the vans careened along Arthur Godfrey Road across the causeway to Miami in a seemingly endless stream.

On 17th Street between Washington and Collins Avenue opposite a main entrance to the Convention Hall, hundreds of youths faced a wall of troopers at about 7 p.m. They chanted "Fight back" and shouted to the delegates entering the hall. "Nixon is a murderer. Stop the B-52s."

With no warning to disperse, the Florida troopers advanced toward the youths. Once again tear gas grenades exploded. The demonstrators scattered across a parking lot, wiping their faces in an attempt to remove the burning, choking, blinding gas clinging to their skin. The gas spread onto the convention grounds and seeped into the convention arena. Scores of delegates and media workers rushed to the lavatories, washing their faces. Others sought relief in the first aid stations in the convention halls.

On 17th Street, a black Cadillac limousine filled with delegates crashed at a high speed into the demonstrators. One young girl was seriously injured when a wheel rolled over her right leg. In a rage, the demonstrators attacked the limousine, pounding on its sides with their bare fists. The right front tire of the limousine blew, and the limousine halted abruptly.

Police charged into the youths, scattering them with their clubs, and escorting the well-dressed delegates to the convention gate. The limousine, its tire flattened, its sides dented, was abandoned in the parking lot.

A yellow cab carrying delegates also ran over five youths on Collins Avenue. The youths were carried off in screaming ambulances.

The Battle of Palm Beach County Continues
People's Weekly World

November 18, 2000

WEST PALM BEACH, Florida—Sitting at a table outside the county's Emergency Operation Center, the three-member Palm Beach County canvassing board voted unanimously to resume the hand count of all 462,657 ballots cast in the November 7 presidential election.

The decision by Court Judge Charles Burton, County Commissioner Carol Roberts and Elections Supervisor Theresa LePore was a defiant rebuff to Florida Secretary of State Katherine Harris, who set a 5 p.m. deadline for the certification of vote totals from all sixty-seven Florida counties.

(The status of the election in Florida changes so quickly that it is impossible to report on all the twists and turns. At press time, Harris had announced she was rejecting the written justifications for recounts, which had been submitted to her).

Harris, a millionaire citrus heiress, is the chair of the Florida Bush campaign.

Hundreds of Florida trade unionists and voting rights advocates converged on the center to observe the canvassing board meeting.

Bush officials pleaded with the panel to suspend the recount pending a ruling by the Florida Supreme Court. "What happens if we continue the count?" Roberts responded.

"Do we go to jail—because I'm willing to go to jail."

A cheer went up from the crowd packing the parking lot. Judge Burton admonished the crowd to remain silent. "This is not a political rally," he said. "We are trying to conduct this meeting in a professional manner."

The board voted to resume the hand count at 7 a.m. November 15. Democrat Al Gore carried this county in a landslide but more than half the ballots thrown out were in precincts with majority elderly or Black voters.

Florida AFL-CIO President Marilyn Lenard told the *World*: "Liberty, justice, freedom—those are things that all working Florida families believe in. We are here to make sure every vote counts."

She cited mounting evidence of balloting irregularities in several other Florida counties, "especially in predominately African American precincts." In Duvall County, 22,000 ballots were not counted. "There were irregularities in Osceola County," she said. "The problem is not limited to Palm Beach County."

"The solution, is to count every vote," she said, "The voters must not be disenfranchised." She stopped short of charging a conspiracy to steal the presidential election. "We certainly are concerned," she said. "Without making allegations, we need to find out. We need to investigate."

Lenard said Bush is rushing to end the ballot recount and declare himself the winner. "I think it will be very difficult for any presidential candidate to govern if people doubt the fairness of the election or the accuracy of the ballot count," she said.

Tony Fransetta, president of the Florida Council of Senior Citizens and leaders of the state's 25,000-member United Auto Worker Retiree Council, echoed that view. "If Bush becomes president without properly resolving the questions about the vote in Florida, he will carry the stigma for the rest of his life, Fransetta said.

"The people's perception will be that he stole the election. The only way this election can be viewed as fair is to go ahead with a complete hand recount of the vote and resolve the issue of 19,000 disenfranchised voters," he said. "If we don't do that, there will be no closure on the issue."

On November 13, nearly 5,000 protesters marched behind the Reverend Jesse Jackson and other leaders along Flagler Drive to the Palm Beach Government Center.

It was an idyllic afternoon with a warm breeze stirring the royal palms. Sleek yachts were moored along the Intracoastal Waterway and across the bay were the mansions of the Palm Beach super-rich including Donald Trump's castle.

The crowd chanted "Count my vote!" A handful of Bush supporters infiltrated the march and seized all the space directly in front of the speaker's platform. "Jesse go home," they chanted, waving their Bush placards.

It was clearly a well-planned attempt to provoke a violent confrontation, but the marchers refused to be provoked.

After a half-hour standoff the marchers returned to the Meyer Amphitheater where the march began. When the rally reconvened, a Black minister asked that all signs and placards be lowered. Only the Bush agents refused.

Hands reached up, tore the Bush-Cheney posters from their sticks and ripped them to shreds. A cheer went up from the crowd.

"I marched thirty-five years ago in Selma for the right to vote," Jackson thundered.

"We marched too far, bled too profusely, died too young. We must not surrender to those who want to stop us from voting," he said.

"This crisis is not about the presidency. It is about the sanctity of the vote. It is not about Democrats, it is about democracy. It is not about Republicans, it is about the Republic."

Buses descend on Tallahassee to protest Bush-Chenney 'Coup d'etat'
People's Weekly World

Jan. 26, 2001

TALLAHASEE, Florida—Led by civil rights and labor leaders, 4,000 protesters marched to the Florida capitol January 20 in a "Day of Moral Outrage" against George W. Bush's inauguration as 43rd president. As they marched they sang, "Ain't going to let no Bush turn me round."

They came on eighty-five chartered buses, by car and plane from Miami, Fort Lauderdale, West Palm Beach, Orlando, Jacksonville, Tampa, and Gainesville. At least fifteen buses came from Atlanta.

A group of NAACP marchers came from Mississippi and cheers went up when a delegation from Selma, Alabama, birthplace of the voting rights movement, was announced.

Other sponsors included the AFL-CIO, the National Organization for Women, the Black Leadership Forum, Rainbow Coalition/Operation Push and many community groups.

They marched from the civic center on a chilly overcast day carrying hand-lettered placards that proclaimed, "Hail to the thief" and "No racist! No homophobe! No bigot! No Ashcroft," referring to Bush's choice for U.S. Attorney General.

Judy Felder, a Tallahassee social worker, held a sign that read, "George II, selected, not elected." "The Supreme Court's decision to stop counting the votes in Florida was not representative of the people," She told the World. "It's like a mantle passed down from father to son. This is a coronation of King George II, not an inauguration."

Marsha Martin, a nurse from Gainesville, marched with her young daughter Molly. "This is the first demonstration I have attended since the Vietnam war," she said. "But when I saw what was happening in this election, I said to myself, 'This is Nixon all over again!' This is not a Black-white issue. This is class struggle. The rich don't want us to have what they have."

Tony Hill is secretary-treasurer of the Florida AFL-CIO and a former leader of the International Longshoremen's Association in Jacksonville who served in the Florida Legislature. "Out of 945,000 African Americans who were eligible to vote in Florida, 893,000 actually voted, over ninety percent. That is unheard of!" he said. "If all of those ballots had been counted, they would not be swearing Bush in today. We have to put these right-wing legislators out of office, keep the issues out there so that people don't fall into an apathetic mood. We are trying to get some sensible people elected."

The crowd rallied in the courtyard of the handsome Florida Capitol building. Congressional Black Caucus member, Representative Corrine Brown (D-Florida) was one of thirteen lawmakers who walked out of the U.S. House of Representatives when Florida's twenty-five electoral votes were certified for Bush January 5. "What happened in the election will go down in history as a coup d'état, not with guns," she said as the crowd cheered. "We're talking about (Florida Secretary of State), Katherine Harris, Governor Jeb Bush, who stole thousands of votes in Florida."

Also present were State Representative Kendrick Meek and Barbara DeVaine, chair of Florida NOW. Together with Hill, they had staged a twenty-six-hour sit-in in Governor Jeb Bush's office a year ago to protest his "One Florida" scheme that ended affirmative action. That triggered a march by 50,000 on Tallahassee March 6. That, in turn, set the stage for the struggle to defeat Bush-Cheney November 7 and the five-week post-election "battle for Florida."

In her speech, DeVaine invoked the words of Mother Jones, "Pray for the dead and fight like hell for the living." She also quoted abolitionist Frederick Douglass that there is "no progress without struggle . . . thunder and lightning" adding, "We're all in this together. There's no stopping us now. The 'lightning' is what we will do to Jeb Bush in 2002."

AFSCME President Gerald McEntee pointed out that this was the third march on Tallahassee in the past five weeks. "We were cheated and democracy was high-jacked on November 7," he said. "We've got to stay angry, stay engaged. We're going to turn Tallahassee into Montgomery in the summer, in the winter. Together, we are going to reclaim Florida and reclaim America."

Without mentioning Democratic Party Chairman Ed Rendell by name, former Atlanta Mayor Maynard Jackson alluded to his public call for Al Gore to concede to Bush while the battle for Florida was raging. Jackson told the crowd he is campaigning to be the new Democratic Party chairman.

Doctor Joseph Lowery, chair of the Black Leadership Forum, said, "The mean-spirited, retrograde forces that run the Republican Party are now visible but they are not invincible. We have to congratulate ourselves. This coalition of conscience turned out in great numbers in November and won a great victory. Wait until 2002 and 2004!"

NAACP President Kweisi Mfume recalled the *Pledge of Allegiance* recited by schoolchildren every day. "Yet we come to Florida to acknowledge that we are not yet 'one nation, indivisible' nor do we everywhere practice 'liberty and justice for all.' Florida stands as an example of justice denied." On election day, he said, thousands of Florida voters received a recorded telephone message falsely reporting that the NAACP had endorsed Bush, evidence that "things were awry in Florida."

After weeks of NAACP protests of Voting Rights violations, Attorney General Janet Reno sent two investigators who gave Florida a clean bill of health. "If the Justice Department can do what they did to protect Elian Gonzalez, they can come to Florida to protect the right to vote," said Mfume. "While the eyes of the nation are on the inauguration, we remember and we must never forget."

Florida, Engulfed in a World of Pain

Sept. 10, 2004
ARCADIA, Florida—As the people of Florida were digging out from Hurricane Charley August 25, three Marine sergeants arrived at the home of Carlos Arredondo in Hollywood, Florida They were bringing news that would hit Arredondo even harder than a force four hurricane. His son, Lance Corporal Alexander Arredondo, had been killed in Najaf, Iraq.

In bitter grief, the father, a Costa Rican immigrant, retrieved a can of gasoline from his garage, doused the

U.S. government van and set it on fire before the stunned officers could stop him. He suffered burns over twenty-six percent of his body. The Pentagon is not pressing charges even though the van was destroyed. Melida Arredondo, stepmother of the slain soldier, said on *Good Morning America* that her husband's rage "is his

scream that his child is dead. This war needs to stop."

Florida ranks fourth nationwide in the number of Iraq war fatalities. The Arredondo family's tragedy, coupled with two hurricanes in less than a month, is a reminder that the people of Florida are in a world of pain.

Tens of thousands have been left homeless and unemployed, waiting anxiously for massive relief that only the federal government can deliver. Some compare their plight to that of the people of Baghdad waiting for water, food, shelter and electricity. George W. Bush asked for $2 billion to repair the damage from Hurricane Charley even though the cost from that blast was at least $7 billion. Now Hurricane Frances has roared through the state and the official damage estimate for both hurricanes is $40 billion.

Hurricane Charley's mass devastation

Take Emma Martinez, a juvenile justice counselor for the state of Florida. She had joined hundreds at a Red Cross soup kitchen in the parking lot of St. Paul Roman Catholic Church in this devastated farm worker town, located about fifty miles east of Sarasota, one afternoon.

She told the *World* her husband had just brought her home from the hospital, still hurting from surgery, the evening Hurricane Charley struck. "It was blowing so hard we couldn't get out of the pickup truck so we just kept on driving to the shelter," she said.

Hundreds had taken refuge, packed like sardines in the main meeting hall. "Thirty minutes after we arrived, the roof lifted up and was gone. The wind and rain came in. People panicked and stampeded over me. I was still in pain and vomiting. Red Cross workers came in and rescued me." They took her to another shelter that was also barely holding together against the tempest. "I went back to my house a week and a half later," she said. "The roof was badly damaged. All my furniture and carpets were soaked."

Martinez said she had to buy a portable generator with her own money even though the federal government claims it is providing vouchers to buy the generators for thousands of families still without power. "At least my house is still standing. My neighbors, mostly farm workers, lived in mobile homes that were destroyed. How could we turn them away? We have two other families living with us whose homes were completely wiped out."

Immigrants and poor hit especially hard

Martinez had brought a young mother with her two children to the Red Cross station. "She hopes that Red Cross or Catholic Charities will provide her some financial assistance because the federal government is denying funds to immigrants," Martinez said. "Many more migrant farm workers will start arriving home from up north where they were following the harvest. But eighty percent of the citrus crop has been destroyed. They will have no jobs. If the federal government is denying assistance to those who are here already, what hope is there for these families who come back in the fall?"

Sitting nearby was Joe Guzman, a disabled farm worker whose mobile home, a rental property, was destroyed. "I am staying in my landlord's house. There are five of us and he is charging each of us $100 a month," Guzman said in Spanish. "But I have no money because there is no work."

A few blocks away, just off Martin Luther King Avenue, the homes of African American families were destroyed. "This is living hell," said one resident, Marshall Smith. "I've been here many years and I have never seen devastation like this. Bush thinks he will get a second term but I don't think he will. His brother was down here promising money to rebuild but we've already been waiting too long. George W. Bush is a crook. He wants everything for himself and his rich friends."

Smith showed this reporter his Veterans Administration ID. "I spent two years, six months and two days in the Army in Germany. I'm a veteran so it makes me angry that they would lie about John Kerry's war record. He earned his medals."

Price gouging and insurance swindles

It remains to be seen whether the Bush brothers will keep those promises. Everything will be off after November 2, if Bush steals a second term. The Federal Emergency Management Administration (FEMA) promised relief to victims of Hurricane Isabel last year. But thousands up and down the Atlantic seaboard never received a dime. The Florida attorney general has reported thousands of cases of price gouging and other swindles inflicted on the suffering people.

Allstate and State Farm Insurance, the two largest property insurance companies serving Florida, have connived with Florida officials to leave thousands of hurricane-battered homeowners holding the bag, according to a front page exposé in the September 7 *Wall Street Journal* (WSJ). In 1992, WSJ reports, State Farm and Allstate paid out a combined total of $6.2 billion for damage inflicted by Hurricane Andrew. But after Hurricane Charley, they paid out only $625 million, ten percent of their 1992 liability, even though the cost of construction has obviously soared in the past twelve years.

The *WSJ* said the shift is the result of "a decade of maneuvering by insurance companies and state officials that has dramatically reduced the obligations of private insurers to pay for the impact of catastrophic storms." The changes include 400 percent increases in premiums and deductibles quietly implemented when the insurance companies threatened to dump 1.2 million homeowners after Hurricane Andrew. Florida officials agreed to "shift from insurance companies to consumers the burden of paying hundreds of millions of storm related losses," *WSJ* charged. The insurance companies long ago stopped covering flood damage in Florida, one of the main sources of the hurricanes' destruction.

Mac Jones, fifty-three, a mailman in Belle Isle south of Orlando, told the *WSJ* his insurance company told him he must pay a 5.3 percent deductible or $6,200 to repair damage to his home. "This is legalized price gouging. They are ripping me off," Jones said.

Labor mobilizes to give helping hand

By contrast, thousands of volunteers and other relief workers have flooded in to help the people, motivated not by profit greed but solidarity. The AFL-CIO and its affiliates have been among the most generous.

Al Dudzinski, an assembly line worker at GM's Saturn plant in Spring Hill, Tenn., rushed to Florida with three other members of the United Auto Worker Local 1853 Disaster Response Team. The *World* interviewed him at the Red Cross command center in Bradenton, Florida

"Too many people have the perception that the labor movement is just about wages and contracts," Dudzinski said. "It's not. We all experience disasters and setbacks and need neighbors who will reach out and lend a helping hand. Unions are among the first to respond but they don't advertise it that much. I think we should. The labor movement gets a bad rap. But we are trying to raise the living standards for everyone."

Dudzinski looked weary after several days of relief work. "We've been sleeping on the floor of this center," he said. "That's fine. We're not here for our personal comfort. We're here to help. We are not the ones who have lost everything."

Keith Ebert, another UAW Local 1853 volunteer, interjected, "Big Business isn't going to do that. That's why we're here. We were delivering food and water one day and a little girl came up and said, 'Thank you for helping us.' That made it all worthwhile. Disasters affect everyone. It doesn't matter whether you are union or nonunion, rich or poor, young or old, Black, Latino or white. We're human beings and we've got to stick together."

Solidarity runs deep

Carl Askew, the AFL-CIO's liaison with the Red Cross, is a veteran of many disasters. Based in Columbus, Ohio, he was one of those who volunteered for duty in New York City within hours of the September 11, 2001 terrorist attack. "The Red Cross was trying to find space in lower Manhattan. We found a CWA union hall within one block of ground zero," he said. "It didn't cost the Red Cross a penny. New York is 100 percent unionized. I had two IBEW electricians assigned to the effort all the time. We had unionized elevator mechanics, union carpenters—all union hardhats. My job was to make sure they had what they needed."

Kelly Reffett, who serves as liaison with the Red Cross for the Chicago AFL-CIO Central Labor Council, said immediate response to humanitarian crisis is "second nature" for union men and women. "Usually the first union I call is the Teamsters because there are always transport needs," she said. "They always respond within a minute's notice. They are overwhelmingly generous. When 9/11 struck, all our Red Cross communications equipment was down in Nashville. We called the Teamsters. They and UPS responded immediately, rushing our equipment up to New York."

Highly visible are the utility lineman with their fleets of cherry picker rigs enduring the heat, humidity, and daily tropical downpours to get electricity service in

Florida restored. Most are members of the International Brotherhood of Electrical Workers (IBEW).

James Romine was one of seventy-six linemen employed by the Dillard Construction Company of Chattanooga, Tenn. A member of IBEW Local 760, he was toiling to restore power in Port Charlotte. "We've got every rig we could muster in here," he told the *World.* "It's really bad. It's so hot and humid and every afternoon the rain pours. We're here until we get the job done. We've been through a lot of storms, Hugo, Andrew, an ice storm in Kansas City. We know what we're doing saves lives and makes life livable for everyone."

Unclear impact on the November 2 vote

Governor Jeb Bush skipped the GOP convention in New York, hoping to harvest a bumper crop of votes by orchestrating the relief efforts around Hurricane Charley. And the strategy seemed to be going well. Then Hurricane Frances struck the Sunshine State a second deadly blow. Now there are concerns that the devastation will make it that much harder to open enough polling places for the homeless thousands to insure a fair election with every vote counted.

Tony Fransetta, president of the Florida Alliance of Retired Americans, speaking before Hurricane Frances hit, told the *World* that it is too early to tell how the hurricane will affect Florida voters given the immensity of the humanitarian crisis. The misery is mounting and with it anger and frustration that so much is being squandered on needless war and tax gifts to the rich while human needs are unmet.

"Up until the Iraq war, I always supported the commander in chief," said Fransetta, a Korean War vet. "But Iraq was a case of George W. Bush putting together myths and lies to justify a war on a nation that never killed a single American. This was a war of retribution, a war for oil. Florida is a battleground state. They keep trying to take it and we keep saying, 'No!' We won it last time and we're going to win it again November 2."

Portraits of Harriette and Harry Moore. Courtesy of DeLaura Junior
High School, Multicultural Research Project, 12/25/95

The Sacrifice of Harry & Harriette Moore
People's Weekly World

February 24, 2001

WEST PALM BEACH--If Florida NAACP organizer Harry
T. Moore had been alive last year, it is a safe bet that he
would have been in the thick of the NAACP's "get out the
vote" drive in the Sunshine State.

That NAACP drive brought a record-smashing 843,000
Black voters to the polls in Florida. They voted overwhelmingly against George W. Bush.

The NAACP, AFL-CIO, and other progressive groups
were so successful that the Bush-Cheney campaign was
forced to turn to the ultra-right majority on the U.S.
Supreme Court to halt the vote count and steal the election for Bush.

Moore's daughter, Juanita Evangeline Moore, sees
a clear parallel between her father's pioneering voting
rights drive fifty years ago and the anti-Bush outpouring last November 7. Her father, she told the *World* in a
telephone interview from her home in Maryland, had directed a voter registration drive that signed up thirty-one
percent of Florida's Black voters, fifty percent more than
in any other southern state.

This was an astounding achievement at a time when
the racist poll tax, literacy tests and KKK terror excluded
millions of Black voters across the south.

"My father seized on a Supreme Court ruling in Smith verses Allwright that Blacks could no longer be excluded from registering as Democrats or from voting in the Democratic primary," she explained.

"When that ruling was handed down, Daddy tried to change his registration from Republican to Democrat in Brevard County. Of course, he got the runaround."

Moore wrote a letter to Florida Attorney General Tom Watson, asking his office to instruct election supervisors throughout the state to follow the Supreme Court ruling.

Moore was so determined that he established an organization called the Progressive Voters League (PVL) of Florida. It enrolled 100,000 members across the state, a powerhouse of independent political action.

Finally, in the 1948 election, African Americans were able to register and vote in the Democratic primary.

"It was a long struggle. People would show up at the courthouse to try to register and they were just brushed off," Evangeline Moore said.

"The excuses given were exactly like what happened in Palm Beach County, Miami-Dade, and eight other Florida counties in the election last November."

Moore and his wife, Harriette, were grievously wounded in a bomb blast as they slept in their modest house outside Mims, Florida Christmas night 1951.

Klansmen had placed the bomb under the bedroom of the modest bungalow. It was also their twenty-fifth wedding anniversary.

In that era of racist segregation, there was no ambulance that would carry Harry and Harriette to a hospital so her two brothers drove them. Harry died in his mother's arms on the way to the hospital in Sanford, thirty miles away. Harriette lingered for nine days, insisting on being taken to Harry's funeral.

Their supreme sacrifice was practically forgotten for half a century. Now, at long last, the Moores are being honored as heroes.

Author Ben Green has written a biography, *Before His time: The Untold Story of Harry T. Moore, Americas First Civil Rights Martyr* (Free Press, 1999).

"He was registering Black voters and organizing Black citrus workers. That's what got him killed. . . ." Green argues in his book.

The University of Florida's Documentary Institute produced a ninety-minute film, *Freedom Never Dies: The Legacy of Harry T. Moore*, which aired on PBS in February.

It featured a moving interview with Evangeline, their only surviving child.

"It is quite gratifying to see that my parents are finally being recognized," Moore said. "I think it was all covered up by the state of Florida, a tourist state that didn't want people to see the evil truth." Nobody was ever arrested for their murder.

"My dad actually was the first martyr of the civil rights movement," Moore said. "The work he did laid the foundation for the civil rights movement that was to come. He fought for equal rights for everyone."

As director of the Florida NAACP during the 1930s and 1940s, Harry, often with Harriette at his side, crisscrossed the state in his car recruiting new members. He was also an educator and organized the Florida State Teachers Association, which filed a lawsuit that overturned the racist wage differential in which Black teachers were paid half the salaries of white teachers.

He crusaded against lynchings, a grisly, genocidal crime in which Florida ranked first in the nation.

In a 1947 letter to members, Moore exulted, "One year ago there were sixty-one branches of the NAACP in our state. Today, Florida has seventy-eight branches. Just think how many innocent Negroes whose lives have been saved by the legal machinery of the NAACP."

The "Groveland Four" were four young Black men framed in 1949 on charges of raping a white woman outside the town of Groveland, Florida. They were savagely and repeatedly beaten in an unsuccessful attempt to force them to confess.

It was called the "Little Scottsboro Case" after the 1930 frame-up of eight Black youth in Scottsboro, Ala. Only a decades-long battle saved the Scottsboro defendants from the electric chair.

In the Groveland case, Charlie Greenlee, sixteen, Samuel Shepherd, twenty-two, Walter Irvin, twenty-two, and Ernest Thomas, were accused of the rape. Police arrested the first three but Thomas fled. He was tracked down by a lynch mob that shot him to death. It took an all-white jury two hours and one minute to find the other three defendants guilty.

Shepherd and Irvin were sentenced to death while Greenlee received a life sentence even though a physician who examined the woman could not determine that she had been raped.

With the NAACP providing the legal defense, the appeal went all the way to the U.S. Supreme Court, which found such outrageous judicial misconduct by the State of Florida that it ordered a new trial.

On the night of November 6, 1951, Lake County Sheriff Willis McCall, a white supremacist, took Shepherd and Irvin from the Florida Penitentiary in Raifors on the pretext of transporting them to the site of a new trial.

He stopped the vehicle on a lonely road, ordered the two handcuffed young men out and shot them each three times. A deputy arrived and noticed Irvin still moving. He shot him again.

Shepherd died but Irvin survived by playing dead. He became a devastating witness, exposing McCall as a cold-blooded racist murderer. Nevertheless, an all-white grand jury exonerated McCall on grounds of "self-defense."

He served as Lake County Sheriff until Governor Reubin Askew suspended him in 1972 after he was indicted for murder.

Irvin was tried again and sentenced to death. Moore plunged into the struggle to save the Groveland defendants. He set out on a speaking tour along Florida's east coast to raise money for the defense and to demand that Sheriff McCall and his cohorts be fired and prosecuted for Shepherds murder.

On December 2, 1951, Moore wrote to Florida's white supremacist governor, Fuller Warren, warning, "Florida is on trial before the rest of the world. Only prompt and courageous action by you in removing these officers can save the good name of our fair state."

Three weeks later, Moore died in the bomb blast. Henriette was mortally wounded. Evangeline was an employee of the U.S. Labor Department in Washington and was aboard a train heading home to spend Christmas with her family when the heinous crime was committed.

She did not learn that her father was dead until she arrived at the railroad station in Mims.

Stetson Kennedy, author of *Southern Exposure, The Klan Unmasked* and other exposes of white supremacist groups, played a major role in keeping alive the case of the Groveland frame-up and the double murder of the Moores. A native of Jacksonville, Florida, Kennedy flatly charged that the U.S. Justice Department, the FBI, as well as Florida law enforcement agencies engaged in a "whitewash" of the Groveland and Moore murders.

In 1981, Kennedy launched a crusade, based on Klansman Raymond Henrys confession that he made the bomb that killed the Moores. Henry accused McCall of planning the assassination.

Kennedy is a skilled investigative journalist who helped prepare the famous "We Charge Genocide" petition presented to the United Nations in November 1950 by Paul Robeson and William L. Patterson, leaders of the Civil Rights Congress (CRC).

Kennedy had infiltrated the Klan and provided much of the voluminous evidence in that indictment of the lynchings, beatings and other racist crimes committed against African Americans.

Prominent in the cases cited in the petition was that of the Groveland Four.

"I think it was Moore's role in exposing the Groveland frame-up that sealed his fate," Kennedy told the *World* from his home in Jacksonville, Florida.

"Sheriff Willis McCall emptied his pistol into those two young prisoners. He had promised the Klan that he would reverse the Supreme Court," he said.

"Moore was very active, investigating the many lynchings and the dozen bombings that occurred in Florida. He was demanding that McCall be fired.

"That, together with his program of total equality, was enough for the white supremacists to kill him."

Kennedy said Moore was a man of strong political independence.

In 1950, incumbent Senator Claude Pepper, a staunch New Deal Democrat, faced a vicious, redbaiting challenge from George Smathers, a diehard segregationist, in the Democratic primary.

Despite strenuous support from Moore, the PVL, labor and other progressive forces, Pepper lost. Kennedy decided to run for the seat as an independent.

Moore invited the Republican candidate and Kennedy to address a PVL conference. The Republican didn't show up, but Kennedy did.

"They endorsed me unanimously and proceeded to blanket Florida with leaflets urging a vote for me," Kennedy said.

But when the votes were counted, Smathers won. Kennedy's vote total was 813 even though the PVL had 100,000 members.

"Things have not changed much in Florida. They still refuse to count votes," Kennedy said with a chuckle.

The Moore assassination sent shock waves across the country and around the world. NAACP Executive Secretary Walter White came to Mims to denounce the murders. Other human rights groups also responded.

The December 27, 1951 edition of the *Daily Worker* carried a banner headline, *NAACP Aide Killed by Bomb in Florida Reign of Terror*. The paper sent reporter Joseph North to cover the double murder.

The CRC sent a delegation to Moore's funeral that included many top leaders of the Congress of Industrial Organizations (CIO). The St. James Missionary Baptist Church in Mims was filled to overflowing.

Later, when an all-white jury sentenced Irvin to death in his second trial, both the NAACP and the CRC called for mass protest rallies across the nation.

CRC Chairman William L. Patterson called Irvin's death sentence "one of the most shocking acts of genocide against the Negro people yet committed by a state government in the U.S. since the United Nations adoption of the convention on genocide."

The defense movement eventually won commutation of Irvin's sentence to life in prison. In 1969, he was finally pardoned. He died a year later.

Clarence Rowe, president of the Central Brevard County branch of the NAACP, is also the chairman of the committee that is working to restore the memory of Harry and Harriette Moore. A new Brevard County courthouse is named, "The Harry T. and Harriette V. Moore Courthouse"

The town of Fellsmere, Florida has scheduled a ribbon cutting for a community center also named for the Moores. There are also plans to commission a bronze statue of the couple.

Brevard County bought the old Moore family homestead. The state legislature approved $700,000 to build a replica of the Moore house on the site.

A playground, a pavilion and an interpretive center are planned so that a new generation can learn of the Moore's struggle and sacrifice.

In 1991 Governor Lawton Chiles ordered the Moore murder case reopened. But Governor Jeb Bush has done nothing to follow through.

Rowe said the truest memorial to the Moores is to fight for the causes they died for, including the right to vote and have those votes counted.

"We are focused on getting people registered to vote and getting them to the polls next election day," Rowe told the World.

"If we are able to remove Governor Jeb Bush from office in the 2002 election, the rest of the political agenda will follow."

Demand Grows: Free Sami Al-Arian, Repeal Patriot Act!
By Tim Wheeler

Dec. 16, 2005

TAMPA, FL.-- THE REFUSAL OF a twelve-member jury in Tampa, Florida, December 6 to convict Dr. Sami Al-Arian of any of the fifty-one "terrorism" charges against him was another in a string of defeats for the Bush Administration in its use of the Patriot Act in witch-hunt trials.

"There was no evidence to support the charges against him," said the Reverend Sharon Streater, a peace and justice leader who stood with Al-Arian, his wife Nahla, and their five children throughout the two years he has been in prison and five months on trial. "The Justice Department should just let it go! Stop persecuting this man and his family," Streater told the *World.*

Cheers erupted in an overflow hearing room in the federal courthouse in Tampa when the jury foreman read the verdict. Moments later, a crowd of more than 100 family and friends gathered on the courthouse steps to celebrate the stunning victory. "Not a single guilty verdict," exclaimed his lawyer, Linda Moreno. "I have to say, that was more 'not guilty' verdicts in those twenty minutes than I've heard in my twenty-five years as a defense attorney."

The jury found Al-Arian, a permanent resident of the U.S., innocent of eight criminal charges including that he belonged to a front group that funneled financial contributions to "terrorists" in Palestine. They also found him not guilty of perjury and immigration violations.

But after deliberating for thirteen days, the jury deadlocked on the nine remaining counts. Two jurors refused to join the majority in finding Al-Arian innocent of all charges.

Just last month, the Justice Department was forced to drop its designation of Jose Padilla as an "enemy combatant." They announced that Padilla, a U.S. citizen, will be tried on charges far less serious than the "dirty bomb" plot announced by then-Attorney General John Ashcroft two years ago. The Justice Department has dropped "terrorism" charges against virtually all the detainees rounded up under the Patriot Act. They are now being tried for routine violations of their immigrant status.

In a telephone interview, his wife, Nahla, told the *World*, "It's a big victory. I saw Sami yesterday and he feels vindicated. He said all along if he could get a fair trial and not be tried in the newspapers, he would be acquitted. The real heroes were the jurors. It took a lot of courage to come up with this verdict. They stood up to the fear and intimidation that our government has imposed since 9/11."

She was deeply disappointed that her husband and the three other defendants, Sameeh T. Hammoudeh, Ghassan Ballut, and Hatim Fariz, did not win full acquittal. "Only two jurors held out. The other jurors complained that these two could not give them any reason for not joining in acquittal."

She voiced anger that he is still in prison. "I am anxious. I don't know what will happen now," she said. "But I hope things will be better than before. Our lawyers are going to file papers asking that he be released." The Justice Department, enraged by the defeat, is now weighing whether to re-try Al-Arian and the other defendants or seek their deportation.

Their case rested on 20,000 hours of FBI wiretaps of Al-Arian's phone conversations many pursuant to the Patriot Act. Al-Arian was fired from his job as a professor of computer science at the University of South Florida (USF) in 2003 for his outspoken defense of Palestinian statehood. His brother in law, also employed at USF, was deported. Al-Arian has spent two years in solitary confinement at a nearby federal penitentiary.

Dwight Lawton, president of the Tampa Bay chapter of Veterans for Peace attended many days of the trial and was present when Arian was acquitted. "The government was looking for an opportunity to get Sami al-Arian," he told the *World*. "I think the events of 9/11 and the Patriot Act emboldened the Bush Administration. They thought 9/11 had enflamed public opinion against the Muslim community and they could empanel a jury that would convict him." The verdict, he said, proved that the people embrace freedom of speech. The repressive sections of the Patriot Act that menace the Bill of Rights, "should be repealed," he said.

Streater echoed that view. "This case is a test of the First Amendment," she said. "Do we believe in our own Constitution? Obviously the jurors did. Sami was an outspoken defender of Palestinian rights and they upheld his right to be outspoken."

David Cole, a Georgetown University law professor who represented Al-Arian's brother-in-law said the Justice Department has no grounds to deport Al-Arian. "At the end of the day, you're trying to deport a permanent resident who has not been convicted of any crime based on his political affiliations alone," Cole said. "That raises serious Constitutional questions."

Postscript: Many months after I wrote the story above, Sami Al-Arian finally won his freedom, but not completely. A condition of his release from prison was that must leave the United States immediately. He and his wife, Nahla, now live in Istanbul.

Chapter 7

A Nation of Immigrants . . .

Give me your tired, your poor
Your huddled masses yearning to breathe free
The wretched refuse of your teeming shore
Send these, the homeless, tempest-tost to me
I lift my lamp beside the golden door.

—Emma Lazarus, The New Colossus

Those stirring lines from Emma Lazarus' poem are inscribed at the base of the Statue of Liberty. They are often quoted as words that describe best one of the nation's deepest held values: That the United State is a refuge from oppression, that we are a nation of immigrants. Millions were brought here against their will in chains, others were fleeing religious and political repression, and millions more emigrated here seeking freedom from starvation and homelessness.

Yet billionaire Donald Trump, pours out a torrent of hatred, vowing to deport 11 million undocumented children, women, and men. He vows to build a wall to keep out Mexicans whom he slanders as "rapists" and "criminals."

It does not mean that the words in Emma Lazarus's poem are untrue. It means that we must struggle to reaffirm the values of the poem just as we waged a Civil War to reaffirm the Declaration of Independence with its "self-evident" truth that we are "created equal" and "endowed by our Creator with certain inalienable rights." Until slavery was abolished, those mighty words were hypocrisy.

The struggle to win reform of our immigration laws, to halt the mass deportation, to stop the militarization of our borders, to provide a path to citizenship for those 11 million people is a struggle to reaffirm Emma Lazarus's poem.

In recent years, the mass exodus of up to one million refugees fleeing terrorist repression in the Middle East has been headline news. The Germans have pledged to accept 800,000 of these refugees. How many will the United States accept? If the Republican right is permitted to block the acceptance of refugees from this crisis, it exposes the words in Emma Lazarus' poem as cynical double-talk. Read a few of my stories covering this struggle.

Asian-American unionists step up fight for equality
People's World

August 19, 2007
WASHINGTON—APALA, one of the AFL-CIO's "affinity groups"—along with the Coalition of Labor Union Women, the A. Philip Randolph Institute, the Coalition of Black Trade Unionists, the Labor Council for Latin American Advancement, and Pride at Work—brought hundreds of trade unionists to Washington for their convention, to celebrate their struggles and to chart a path for further advances and victory for working families in 2008.

That election goal is in line with the aims of the national AFL-CIO and the other affinity groups. The federation is laying ambitious plans to expand pro-worker numbers in Congress and to retake the White House.

One theme of APALA's convention was "Living the Legacy," saluting the centuries-long struggle of Asian American and Pacific Islander workers against racist oppression and super-exploitation. But another was implementing the resolution adopted at the AFL-CIO's 2005 convention, to improve racial and gender diversity in union leadership.

APALA President Maria Somma told the delegates the group has tripled in membership since it was founded fifteen years ago. There are now more Asian-Pacific American union organizers, she said, "due in large part to our partnership with the AFL-CIO Organizing Institute." Participants included Change to Win delegates and AFL-CIO members.

Like the rest of organized labor, Somma continued, APALA "has seen the decline in union membership, stagnant wages, disappearing pensions, massive job losses and eroding health care benefits. Unrestricted free market policies are wreaking havoc on workers and benefiting only corporate executives and the wealthy."

Christine Chen, executive director of Asian-Pacific Islander Vote, said the group's voter clout is increasing. In Washington state, Democrat Christine Gregoire won the race for governor by only 146 votes last November. Asian American and Pacific Islander votes were her victory margin, Chen said.

In Virginia, GOP Senator George Allen's use of a racist slur—against an American whose parents emigrated from India—galvanized Asian-American voters, who voted seventy-six percent for Democratic victor Jim Webb. Webb's win gave Democrats control of the Senate.

Yet the Asian-American vote still lags, Chen said: "We need to educate voters not only to get out and vote but to insist that candidates support our interests and our values."

Glenn Magpantay of the Asian-American Legal Defense and Education Fund said Asian-American voters in 2006 "faced discrimination, racial profiling and harassment" similar to Republican vote suppression tactics against others in 2000. Even so, "Asian-Americans voted for change just as voters in general voted for change," he said.

And Asian-Americans supported "legalization of undocumented immigrants and reducing immigration backlogs while they opposed making undocumented a crime," Magpantay said. Legislation legalizing undocumented workers fell victim to a GOP Senate filibuster this year.

AFL-CIO Political Director Karen Ackerman called the 2008 elections an opportunity "to shift the obscene imbalance of power going to the corporations while workers are losing out." Yet, she warned "the Democrats have not made the sale. This is not going to be a slam-dunk." She repeated that warning to union leaders gathered in Chicago.

And she also noted that Democrats are not automatically pro-worker, citing NAFTA as an example. In 1993, when the House, Senate and White House were all in Democratic hands, passage of NAFTA produced devastating consequences for worker, she said. The "strategic goal" for workers is a political realignment "to establish a long-term progressive, pro-worker, pro-union political environment in this country."

At a town hall meeting featuring panelists from the other constituency groups, their leaders echoed several of the themes APALA delegates discussed.

Randolph Institute President Richard Womack addressed the need for more action to have labor's leadership reflect diversity of membership. "We must go back to our local unions and ask: 'What are you doing to implement (the) resolution?' If you don't get involved, make a push, it isn't going to happen. We want to look at the leadership of the labor movement in years to come and say: 'We have won a seat at the table.'"

LCLAA Executive Director Gabriela Lemus said solving job loss created by anti-worker trade policy "will not be by building walls along our borders but by addressing the underlying crisis of unemployment generated by NAFTA." The key to winning in 2008, she said, is "coalition-building, reaching out, working at ground level to build it up."

And CLUW Executive Director Carol Rosenblatt stressed how the Iraq War helped swing women into the 2006 victory coalition. "Our campaign against the war in Iraq was decisive. The war in Iraq impacts everybody, women and their families and we plan to continue pressing that issue," she said, drawing a big round of applause.

"as one people, one more time.

Denver March Urges Dems Back Immigrant Rights
People's World

August 2008
DENVER—Thousands of protesters marched through Mile High City August 28 chanting "Immigrant rights are human rights" and "Hey, hey, ho, ho, John McCain has got to go!"

They carried hundreds of signs and banners supporting Barack Obama for president and denouncing the dragnet arrests, criminalization and deportation of undocumented immigrant workers by Immigration and Customs Enforcement (ICE). The march and rally was sponsored by the "We Are America DNC March & Rally For Immigrant Rights," a broad coalition of labor, religious organizations and other groups working for immigrant rights.

The crowd assembled at a park on Denver's majority Mexican American west side and marched on a freeway to Lincoln Park downtown with hundreds of motorists honking their horns and flashing the victory sign in sympathy.

The march came on the last day of the Democratic National Convention; among the marchers were DNC delegates like former Denver Mayor Federico Peña who walked in the vanguard of the vast crowd. "It's important that all of us as Americans defend the rights of immigrant workers," he told the *World*. "They have come here to work and sustain their families and the economy."

The next president, and the Congress, he added, "must pass comprehensive immigration reform so people can come out of the shadows. Immigrants are coming to our country and making contributions today just as they did for the past two centuries."

The We Are America platform urged the DNC to support "just and fair immigration reform," to stop the criminalization of immigrants; pass the "Dream Act" that permits children of undocumented families to attend college; to stop building walls on the U.S.-Mexican border; stop the "deaths in the desert" and end the ICE raids.

Marlinda Mendoza, a Denver resident, pushed a stroller carrying two of her five children. "We're all equal. We need the same rights as everyone else," she told the

World. "We're hard workers. We don't deserve the laws that are in force today that treat workers like criminals. A lot of my family has been affected by these raids. Children come home from school and their parents are gone, arrested and deported."

The Agape International Spiritual Center & Choir, a multiracial singing group based in Culver City, California, sang the opening night of the DNC. They joined the immigrant rights march singing *The Morning Chant*. Choir Director, Reverend Carolyn Wilkin, told the World, "We're sending a message of love, peace and harmony in the world. We are a multicultural, diverse, spiritual organization and we know we are all united."

"Viva Obama" with several chapters from Oakland to San Diego walked behind their banner. Vicente Rodriguez said, "We like Obama a lot better than McCain. McCain backed off saying that he supports immigration reform. He said 'Security comes first, comprehensive immigration reform second.' But we know that issues left to 'second' never get done."

He sharply assailed the ICE raids. "They are terrorizing communities, not only the undocumented but the documented as well. These raids are taking away the breadwinners of families leaving children behind who are U.S. citizens without food and shelter. This is nothing but terrorism."

Cesar Muñoz, a Spanish language teacher at Colorado Mountain College was wearing a mock-German army uniform with the insignia of the Nazi SS on the collar and the initials "ICE" on the cap. "These ICE raids are a violation of Article 16 of the Universal Declaration of Human Rights," he told the *World*. "They are holding people at detention centers. When you are locked up, you lose your human rights." Just then, a TV crew turned its camera on him. Munoz clicked his heels and his arm shot up in a "Seig heil" salute.

Ivonn Cruz was holding a sign "Nuestra voz es nuestra voto!" She too was marching with her children. "I am a member of Local 14 of Unite-HERE," she told the *World*. "I work at the Hyatt Regency, a union hotel in Denver." She said her sign reflects "that a lot of Latinos are now registered to vote. We broke records. We will make a difference in this election. The people are ready for change. I think Obama is the right person to lead the country."

Chapter *8*

People and Nature Before Profits

More than ever before I am writing about the grave new dangers posed by globalization—global climate change, the looming worldwide food deficits, pandemic disease like HIV-Aids, and antibiotic-resistant strains of TB, Mersa, and other diseases, the die-off of honeybees, starfish, oysters, meadowlarks, and other creatures great and small, bright and beautiful.

It does not mean that the menace to humanity posed by earlier threats such as the crazed stockpiles of nuclear weapons have gone away. I have written stories, marched in demonstrations demanding the total abolition of nuclear weapons.

No, these new threats to the survival of life on earth are added on top of the nuclear peril.

More than ever humanity faces a choice: Are we going to abolish nuclear weapons? Are we going to shift dramatically away from our dependence on fossil fuels in order to curb global climate change?

Scientists have never before posed these threats in such dire terms. We are pushing toward "tipping points" in the accumulation of greenhouse gases in the atmosphere. We are approaching a point of no return.

As with every other crisis in our society, there is a class dimension to globalization. The crazed resistance from the climate deniers and other rightwing crazies is funded by the Koch Brothers and other oil billionaires who owe their ill-gotten profits to oil, coal, and natural gas. That is why the Communist Party has changed its main slogan from "People Before Profits" to "People and Nature Before Profits."

It remains to be seen if we can mobilize a movement broad enough and powerful enough to defeat the energy monopolies and shift our country and the world to sustainable forms of energy. Certainly, energy conservation should be a natural for socialism, a system that puts the needs of the people—and nature—above profits for the wealthy few.

Strong arguments are being made for sustainable energy and energy conservation by the environmental movement and organizations like the Blue-Green Alliance. Falsely, the energy monopolies claim that their industry is a job creator and that the environmental movement would destroy jobs if they win their demands. They claim the Keystone XL Pipeline, for example, will create jobs. But when examined in depth, it turns out that this pipeline would create only a tiny handful of permanent jobs. In the meantime, the heated tar sand oil would be pumped under high pressure through pipes that run directly over the Ogalalla Aquifer and other precious sources of fresh water.

For every environmental threat, a broad, popular democratic protest movement has sprung up, wildlife organizations fighting to save plants and animals, alternative energy movements demanding a shift to sustainable energy, organizations that fight for clean water, soil, and air, the movement of organic and local farmers fighting agribusiness and factory farming, for the labeling of genetically modified organisms (GMOs).

This movement is a crucial sector of the "all people's front" fighting the domination of our country and the world by the transnational corporate ultra-right. The challenge is to overcome divisions, to convince the labor movement that a green economy has the potential to create tens of millions of well-paying jobs installing the technology to generate billions of kilowatts in sustainable power, to retrofit old buildings and build new ones that conserve huge amounts of energy.

Victory in this struggle would give us a livable planet, thriving wildlife, forests, rivers, lakes, and prairies, a system of food production that insures safe, nutritious food and drink for all. The alternative is a planet devoid of life.

Farmers Crowd D.C. in Parity Parade
Daily World

January 1, 1978
WASHINGTON, January 18—Thousands of farmers across the nation poured into Washington today in a huge protest demonstration to demand 100 percent parity for their produce. The farmers traveled into the capital in a "Parity Parade" consisting of tractors, trucks, pickups and scores of chartered buses from states as far as Texas, Arkansas, Minnesota, Tennessee, Georgia and South Carolina.

The farmers fanned out on Capitol Hill today to visit Congressional offices to demand 100 percent parity, which means the same relationship between prices and production that existed from 1910-1914. This would guarantee a small profit for farmers.

Slogans were pinned to the walls of hotels and their vehicles. "It may be peanuts to Carter, but my farm is my life," said a sign attached to the side of a bus from Houston County, Georgia.

Bergland role hit

Another sign referred to the refusal of Agricultural Secretary Robert Bergland to support 100 percent. It read "Crops will be missin' if Bergland don't listen."

Doug Brown of Mullins, South Carolina raises tobacco, corn and beans. He said, "When we sell corn for a dollar fifty-nine a bushel and the 100 percent parity price would be three dollars and forty-five cents per bushel, then you see that we can't make it."

He pointed out that consumers in the supermarket pay a dollar-ten for five pounds of corn meal, but the corn farmer gets only a few pennies. "Where is the rest going? The middleman is getting it all. The national average on parity is .03 percent. A few more years of this and ninety percent of the farmers are going to go broke," Brown said. He denounced as a lie the Carter Administration claim that 100 percent parity would mean a thirty percent increase in food price.

Ceiling on prices

"We would like to put a ceiling on prices so that it would protect the consumer," he said. "There is no reason why prices should go up more than about three percent."

The farmers here are proud of their fabulous productivity. A sign on one bus said, "One U.S. farmer feeds fifty-six people—Without 100 percent parity we won't be able to feed ourselves."

L.J. West and more than a dozen other cotton farmers from Abernathy, Texas, near Lubbock, told this reporter the income margin has evaporated on their crops and they will be forced out of business unless President Carter orders 100 percent parity.

"A lot of people don't realize that the way things are going now, the family farmer is definitely on the way out unless we get some help," he said. "The monopolies are taking over. These corporations can afford to wait until they have control. Then they will charge the consumer what they want to."

Families to lose farms

West said seventeen farmers in the Lubbock area lost their farms in one week last month because of the declining prices for crops and skyrocketing costs of production.

West said he barely breaks even on his 1,700 acre farm situated in the twenty-five-county high plains of west Texas. The region produced three million bales of cotton last year of the total U.S. production of 14.5 million bales.

Meeting Targets 'Environmental Racism'
People's Weekly World

November 2, 1991
WASHINGTON—Hundreds of African American, Latino, Asian and Native-American activists, angered by the use of their communities as toxic dump sites, convened a summit on "environmental racism" here last weekend.

Sponsored by the United Church of Christ's Commission for Racial Justice, the four-day meeting was the first gathering of its kind. Participants included the Gwich'in people of Alaska, Native-Americans of many tribes, African American leaders from Louisiana's "cancer alley," Asian-Americans from the Silicon Valley and many Latino activists from across the country.

They recessed Friday for a protest march to the Capitol. As he marched, Representative Avery C. Alexander, dean of the Black caucus in the Louisiana Legislature, told me he is fighting two kinds of pollution—chemical emissions from 138 petro-chemical plants between Baton Rouge and New Orleans—"cancer alley"—and an even deadlier toxin, the racist pollution of David Duke. "There is a connection between the two," Alexander said, "because the racists always oppose legislation to clean up the environment."

Senator Paul Wellstone, (D-Minn.) welcomed the crowd to the Capitol. The Senate was debating S-1220, the so-called National Energy Security Act by Senator J. Bennett Johnston (D-La.) to permit oil drilling in the Arctic National Wildlife Refuge, home of the Gwich'in people. "It is a comprehensive energy bill: there is something in it for every oil company," he said. "But it is not respectful of the people [or] the environment."

Gwich'in leader Sarah James said, "To see so many people of many colors come together is a good thing. We all breathe the same air." But she warned against S-1220 and the oil company lust for the Arctic Refuge. "The destruction is still going on. The birds are dying."

United Farmworkers Vice President Dolores Huerta said farmworkers and their children are dying from exposure to herbicides and pesticides. "Unless we who are out there suffering the environmental disaster get together, it will continue to happen."

The Reverend Ben Chavis, the Commission's executive director, told a news conference, "We believe that there is a direct correlation between the disproportionate presence of toxic facilities and pollutants and the increase of infant mortality rates, birth defects, cancer and respiratory illnesses in People of Color communities. This insidious form of institutionalized racism must be challenged and must be stopped."

The Commission released a report in 1987, "Toxic Waste and Race," which revealed that sixty percent of both African American and Hispanic people live in communities with one or more uncontrolled waste sites. The nation's largest hazardous landfill, which serves forty-five states plus several foreign countries, is in Emelle, Alabama, 78.9 percent Black. The predominately African American and Latino South side of Chicago has the greatest concentration of waste sites in the nation. Los Angeles, about thirty percent Latino, is home to fourteen waste sites—thirty-four percent of the sites in California.

Chavis blasted the Environmental Protection Agency for refusing to enforce clean air, ground and water laws. He put members of Congress on notice that they will be held accountable for their failure to oversee EPA enforcement and to enact tougher enforcement laws.

Addressing President Bush, Chavis said, "You have failed to keep your promise . . . It appears to us that the Bush administration has a greater commitment to protect the petrochemical industry and other large corporate interests rather than the environment."

He called for a ban on the Nuclear Regulatory Agency's plans to store nuclear wastes on the lands of the Western Shoshone in Nevada. "We are opposed to any attempts to export toxic wastes from the United States to People of Color communities in Third World countries." Chavis told the World, "In all my years in the civil rights movement, this issue has emerged as one that reaches across the lines of race."

Another reason for the summit is to exert pressure on the mainstream environmental organizations to increase the numbers of African Americans, Latinos and Native Americans in all levels of their organizations, which are overwhelmingly white.

Chavis emphasized that the summit seeks friendly ties and joint action with these groups. "We've invited them to join us as we together redefine environmentalism," he said, "as we pose the question: What social transformations are needed to protect our environment and our communities?"

Jeanne Guana, co-chair of the SouthWest Organizing Project, marched with the banner of her Albuquerque group. "The Pentagon treats us like a military colony," she said. "The nuclear cycle begins here—research and development. Now the cycle is to be completed with the WIPP site for storage of nuclear waste near Carlsbad. We are a 'national sacrifice area.' Only a few brown people live there. We are expendable. We have to rise up for our own survival. Clearly, the protection of beautiful New Mexico is at stake. For 500 years, my family has lived there. I have a responsibility to maintain it for 500 years more."

12,000 Ring White House to Protest Tar Sands Pipeline

By Tim Wheeler

People's World

November 7, 2011

WASHINGTON—An estimated 12,000 tar sands protesters encircled the White House, November 6, chanting, "Stop the pipeline, stop the greed, and give the people what they need."

On a cool, solar-powered autumn afternoon, the demonstrators from as far away as Montana and Nebraska gathered in Lafayette Park near the White House to urge President Obama to deny a permit for TransCanada's proposed 1,700 mile Keystone XL-Pipeline. The $7 billion project would carry tar sand oil from Calgary, Alberta, Canada, to the Gulf Coast of Texas.

Bill McKibben of Vermont, a founder of 350.org, a grassroots organization that is combating global climate change told the crowd, "Four years ago, then candidate Obama said his administration would begin to 'slow the rise of the oceans and heal the planet.' This week scientists announced the greatest-ever annual increase in carbon emissions. We need action to match those words and without Congress in the way, Keystone is the place to start."

NASA's top climate scientist, James Hansen, said a victory in blocking the tar sands pipeline would be a step toward ending "fossil fuel addiction. Either we stop now or we destroy the Earth."

Natural Resources Defense Council founder, John H. Adams, awarded the Presidential Medal of Freedom by Obama, cited reports that the White House may delay approval of the pipeline. "My guess is if there is a delay, it could very well kill the pipeline of its own weight," Adams said.

Alison Cheroff, a classical pianist, who lives in Barre, Vermont, came on one of three chartered buses from the Green Mountain State. "This is such a vital turning point in the survival of the world," she told the *World.*

"We have only a few years to turn it around. We need to shift over to alternative energy on a massive scale. They say it will cost jobs. I think a green economy will create millions of jobs."

The actor, Margot Kidder was one of four women holding a banner that read, "Montana Women for An Oil-Free Future." Kidder owns a home in Livingstone, Montana, which is called the "Gateway to Yellowstone National Park." She was one of more than seventy tar sands protesters arrested in a sit-in outside the White House last August 20.

She told the World a sixteen-inch pipeline broke under the Yellowstone River and flooded both the river itself and adjoining ranchland with crude oil. "Exxon still hasn't cleaned up that mess," she said. "Their clean-up plan is paper towels and baby diapers."

The tar sands pipeline would be thirty-six inches in diameter, she said, "very high pressure, with high heat just to make the oil flow in the pipeline." Rupture of that pipeline would destroy some of the nation's most pristine wilderness, she warned.

TransCanada strong-arms ranchers, she charged. "They offer them a dollar a linear foot to lay the pipeline across their land, claiming 'eminent domain.' If the rancher refuses, TransCanada sues, telling them, 'See you in court in three weeks.'"

She scorned claims that it will create jobs. "These are very temporary jobs, 3,500 to 4,200 by their own estimate. That's about 300 jobs for Montana. It's not worth poisoning the state for that few jobs."

Joseph F. Lado, an analyst at the National Science Foundation said extracting crude oil from tar sands requires vast amounts of natural gas or other energy. "They are talking about building a nuclear power plant to provide the power needed for the refining process, he said. Al Gore said, "A Prius fueled with tar sands gasoline would be more polluting than a Humvee."

Too much of the debate on energy policy is to "end our dependence on foreign oil," he said. "That doesn't answer what the people really want—to shift to renewable energy."

David Freeman served as Chairman of the Tennessee Valley Authority (TVA) under President Jimmy Carter. "During my tenure I shut down eight nuclear reactors that were under construction," he told the *World* as he stood in the crowd. "We had the first solar programs under construction back in those days. Then Reagan came in and declared war on the sun. He ordered the removal of the solar panels Jimmy Carter had installed on the roof of the White House and killed all those solar programs."

Until after World War II, the federally owned TVA "was 100 percent renewable energy" Freeman added. "It wasn't until after the war that TVA started building coal-fired and nuclear powered power stations. We need to make a decision as a nation that fossil fuels are poison. We have the sun, the wind, biomass. We need to make the decision to go to all renewable energy. We're on an energy diet that is killing us."

At Blue-Green Alliance, the Cry Is "Good Jobs, Clean Air"
People's World

May 10, 2010
WASHINGTON—Truck-driver Porfirio Diaz brought the 3,500 delegates at the Good Jobs, Green Jobs national conference here to their feet May 5 with his harrowing story of the struggle he and his fellow drivers are waging for union rights and clean air in the Port of Oakland in California.

Diaz was hired twenty-five years ago as a teamster transporting cargo containers to and from the port, a good union job with living wages and benefits. Then the stevedoring company decreed that the drivers are "independents" paid by the load with no union or health and welfare benefits.

He is not paid when waiting in line to pick up a container nor does he receive overtime pay. He must pay for fuel and maintenance.

"Sometimes I work seventy hours a week and after covering my expenses, I come home with $500," he said. His son suffers acute asthma aggravated by smog generated by the idling trucks in the port. The family fell behind on their mortgage and lost their home in foreclosure.

He told the conference that with help from the labor and environmental movement, the drivers are struggling to pass legislation to win back the benefits they lost and force the companies to reduce port pollution. The crowd was on its feet and Teamster union members led them in chanting, "Good jobs, clean air!"

The conference May 4-6 sponsored by the Blue-Green Alliance was nearly twice as large as last year's gathering. The alliance was founded by the Sierra Club, the Communications Workers of America and the United Steelworkers and now unites more than two dozen unions and environmental organizations.

Speaker after speaker called on Congress and the Obama administration to create millions of new jobs in industries that reduce greenhouse emissions.

United Steelworkers President Leo Gerard cited the explosion at an oil refinery in Anacortes, Washington, that killed six workers, the Massey Energy mine blast that killed twenty-nine, and now the explosion of BP's offshore rig that killed eleven and is spewing millions of gallons of crude into the Gulf.

It shows, he said, "that the labor and environmental issues are connected in many ways."

"Our generation is going to be the one to leave the worst mess in history or . . . the most opportunity in history," he said.

AFL-CIO President Richard Trumka also reminded the delegates of BP's oil well explosion.

"Never before has the need been so urgent to produce clean energy, to use energy more efficiently, to prevent climate change and to protect our natural environment," said Trumka, a former coal miner. "And not since the Great Depression have so many Americans needed new and better jobs with secure benefits," jobs, he said, "that can't be off-shored, downsized or downgraded to part time positions."

Trumka argued that the nation needs coal, oil, nuclear, hydroelectric and wind and solar power but with strict regulations to reduce or eliminate release of carbon dioxide and other gases. He called for insulating existing buildings, a project that save energy and create hundreds of thousands of jobs.

"Tens of thousands of miles of new high-voltage transmission are needed to bring solar, wind, and geothermal power and biofuels," he said.

"It's great news that the Obama administration is providing $8 billion in high-speed rail that will save or create tens of thousands of jobs," Trumka said, but he added, "These jobs need to be American jobs . . . high skill, high wage jobs with safe conditions . . . and the right to be free from discrimination and the right to form and join unions."

House Speaker Nancy Pelosi, D-Calif., said the House-approved Waxman-Markey American Clean Energy and Security Act will "create 1.7 million jobs, reduce our dangerous dependence on foreign oil and cut the pollution that causes global warming."

She declared, "This legislation is an opportunity to transform our economy and create jobs that cannot be shipped overseas . . . It will promote new, clean energy technology - made in America by American workers."

"The House has acted," Pelosi said. "We hope the Senate will act soon." She received a standing ovation.

On the final day, the conference recessed and participants went to Capitol Hill to lobby their senators and representatives for comprehensive clean energy and climate change legislation and for legislation to create millions of jobs.

Midnight thoughts on a lovelorn
mockingbird Baltimore

July 6, 2007

Every night, just after midnight, the mockingbird that resides in the holly tree outside our bedroom window begins to sing. He is so loud, his songs so varied and complex, he wakes me up. I lie there listening to his trills, chirps and long mellifluous melodies.

This must be what happened to the great English lyric poet John Keats. Dying, and unable to sleep one night, he wrote *Ode to a Nightingale* with the lines:

> *Now more than ever seems it rich to die,*
> *To cease upon the midnight with no pain,*
> *While thou art pouring forth thy soul abroad*
> *In such an ecstasy!*

Percy Bysshe Shelley, who also died young, paid homage to the "blithe spirit" of skylarks for filling heaven with "profuse strains of unpremeditated art." Insomnia apparently played a part in the genius of romantic poets.

I will not wax lyrical on the artistry of our mockingbird. Most, if not all, of his songs are plagiarized. His powers of mimicry are so awesome, he can imitate the sirens of approaching fire engines.

This little gray fellow moved into our holly tree here in Baltimore about three years ago, attracted by the thick, thorny foliage, a perfect nesting place. He has been singing his heart out ever since, hoping without success to attract a mate.

Mockingbirds are famous for defending their territory aggressively. Once I saw our mockingbird fluttering frantically against the side of our car parked at the curb. He was charging the side view mirror. Evidently he had caught sight of himself in the mirror and was trying to drive off the intruder.

That was one possible explanation. Another is that he caught sight of himself and imagined it was his long-awaited mate. He was engaged not in combat but in a lovelorn waltz.

I find myself thinking about birds, as well as honeybees, often these days—the canaries in our mine.

A just-released report by the Audubon Society warns, "Since 1967, the average population of the common birds in steepest decline has fallen by 68 percent. Some individual species nosedived as much as 80 percent. All 20 birds on our National Common Birds in Decline List lost at least half their populations in just four decades."

As for honeybees, beekeepers across the country are reporting "empty hive syndrome," the mysterious disappearance of all their bees.

I grew up on a dairy farm in Sequim, Wash. Among my warmest memories are walking across the pastures of our farm in the evening, hearing the joyous song of meadowlarks perched on fence posts. I'd look up and behold dozens of barn swallows swooping gracefully in pursuit of flies and mosquitoes. As for honeybees, they were everywhere in the lush alfalfa and clover or our blooming orchard.

We still own farmland in that valley. Yet it is years since I heard a meadowlark sing. Maybe it's because most of the fence posts are gone as developers build one big McMansion after another on once unspoiled farmland.

The swallows, too, are in steep decline. One reason is that most of the barns have fallen down. And I now watch anxiously for the arrival of honeybees. It seems to me they too are not as plentiful. Our family has made a commitment to keep our 55 acres in farmland, one of only a few parcels of farmland left in our beautiful valley. It is a small step in the struggle against developer greed.

It doesn't do any good to give in to moods of despair. Greg Butcher, the Audubon Society's director of bird conservation, tells us that the culprit in the decline of songbirds is loss of "local habitat and national environmental trends" as well as global climate change.

Saving the birds is "crucial to the well-being of humans as well," Butcher says in an audio message on the

Audubon Society web site. "Only citizen action can make a difference for the birds and the state of our future."

In my youth, the bald eagle had vanished from the Dungeness Valley. Then came Rachel Carson's "Silent Spring," and DDT was banned. Now, we have several nesting pairs of these majestic birds soaring above the Dungeness River on our farm. We are struggling to revive the salmon and steelhead, a staple of their diet, in the Dungeness. Saving the bald eagle is one of the environmental movement's greatest success stories.

And all the news is not bad in Baltimore either. We have a Golden Chain Tree in our front yard. I was standing on the front porch this morning and heard a buzzing among the Golden Chain Tree blooms. The tree was swarming with honeybees. I breathed a little easier.

Epilogue

The author at Barack Obama's acceptance rally, Mile High Stadium, following the Democratic National Convention in Denver, Aug. 28, 2008. The crowd numbered 84,000.

We are the 99%. United We Will Win

In the half century I have been a journalist, I have drawn strength from the courage of the people whose struggles I have covered. They could be flat on their back, slammed to the ground by disasters natural and manmade. Wounded in body and soul, they picked themselves up and moved forward. They found strength in the solidarity of fellow workers, neighbors, friends, and comrades. The working people rushed to the rescue.I think of those miners' wives in Mannington, West Virginia gathered at the Champion Company Store after Consol #9 mine blew up trapping seventy-eight miners. It was the eve of Thanksgiving 1968. I saw the grief and anger in their eyes. They fought back against the Rockefeller-owned Consolidation Coal Company. Those widows and the miners still alive went on to organize the "Black Lung movement" to win benefits for many thousands of miners afflicted with pneumoconiosis. The miners organized "Miners for Democracy" to wrest back the United Mine Workers from class collaborators like Tony Boyle, so deep in bed with the coal companies he murdered Jock Yablonski and his wife and daughter to silence the surging rank and file movement.Solidarity was the secret of the miners' power, an idea expressed by Mother Jones when she said, "Don't Mourn, Organize." And by Florence Reece in her immortal song, "Which Side Are You On?" with the line:

> "Don't scab for the bosses, don't listen to their lies.Us poor folks haven't got a chance unless we organize."

Together we can win not only safer mines, we can also win better pay and benefits. And if we are strong enough, united enough, to win those goals, why not clean water and air, nutritious food, decent housing, education for our children, cradle to grave health care? And if the government refuses to provide those benefits, remove that government from power and replace it with a government that will provide them.

In those immediate, local struggles whether it be a strike, a boycott, a mass rally, or an election campaign, there was the seed of a larger, bolder, more comprehensive change. Call it a grassroots revolution. It is the power of the 99%. We are so powerful we can remove those millionaires and billionaires who squeeze profits from the miners and the rest of us.

There is another folk song I like to sing, *The Banks Are Made of Marble* with the lines, "I have seen the people working/Throughout this mighty land/And I dreamed we'd get together/And together take a stand/Then we'd own those banks of marble/With a guard at every door/And we'd share those vaults of silver/That we all have sweated for."

It's called socialism. I believe in it.

Socialism may not be inevitable but it is surely necessary.

Now in my autumn years, the idea of a profound, democratic change is being discussed widely, thanks in large part to the presidential campaign of Vermont Senator, Bernie Sanders. I have served as co-chair of Clallam County for Bernie Sanders. I have heard the crowds roar their approval of Bernie's speeches calling for a political revolution to overturn our "rigged, corrupt political system" bought and paid for by billionaires like the Koch Brothers.

Yet the millions who have flocked to Bernie Sanders are far, far short of the numbers needed to realize his program. And some of these well-meaning people have turned on Hillary Clinton and Hillary's voters who constituted the clear majority in last November's presidential election beating Donald Trump by about three million votes.

Trump is the most dangerous rightwing extremist president ever to occupy the White House. His campaign slogan was a promise to "make America great again." Yet Trump embodies all that is wrong with America. Like those Roman emperors, Caligula and Nero, his policies, and he himself, are pushing the empire closer to the cliff. If the empire falls, I certainly won't shed tears. Neither should you, dear reader. It is high time our nation stopped being an arrogant global cop. Making our nation a peace loving, good neighbor is one of our biggest responsibilities. If we are not wasting our tax dollars building aircraft carriers, we will have the revenues we need to educate our children and provide health care for every man, woman, and child.

Trump, a billionaire, embodies the yawning gap between the rich and the poor. between the obscenely wealthy one percent and the 99.9%. Working people have suffered a steady decline in income in the past thirty years. The redistribution of wealth from our pockets to theirs is the fundamental contradiction in our society.

That is the reason Trump and the Republicans hate unions so much. The labor movement is fighting to reverse the decline in worker income, pushing for a $15 or even $20 minimum wage, quality health care for all, affordable housing, high quality education K-through-College.

Trump is a bully, a sex predator, a bigot who openly espouses contempt of Mexicans, African Americans, Muslims, women, scientists, unionized workers. He promotes hatred and division, racism in the first place, because he knows that it has been a very successful strategy of the ultra-reactionary ruling elite in our country for over 200 years to preserve their grip on power.

Trump is a militarist. In his current budget, he proposes a staggering $54 billion increase in military spending. Pushing the total to $603 billion. He proposes to spend a trillion dollars in our tax dollars over the next ten years modernizing the U.S. nuclear arsenal. He has appointed John Bolton, an advocate of waging nuclear war, as his National Security Adviser. Trumps reckless, unilateral threats push us toward war, even thermonuclear war.

Trump rejects the warnings of the overwhelming majority of climate scientists that the global temperatures of our planet are rising, triggering catastrophic hurricanes, drought, wildfires, the spread of deserts, rising sea levels, the spread of pandemic diseases. The scientists warn that if we do not act now to reduce greenhouse gases like CO_2, literally billions of people on earth may die. Trump calls it "fake news" and a "hoax" perpetrated by the Chinese.

A majority of the people in our nation voted against Trump in the 2016 election. And opposition to his reactionary policies has skyrocketed. The challenge is to unite all the movements that have been spurred to mass action---the women's equality movement, youth marching against gun violence, "Black Lives Matter," the

DACCA "dreamers", the immigrant communities, the labor movement.

Every story I have written confirms in my mind the truth contained in a slim, 44 page pamphlet my mother handed me when I was 13 years old. It was the Communist Manifesto and its opening lines read:

"The history of all hitherto existing society is the history of class struggles....Freeman and slave, patrician and plebian, lord and serf, guildmaster and journeyman, in a word, oppressor and oppressed, stood in constant opposition to one another, carried on an uninterrupted, now hidden, now open fight, a fight that ended, either in a revolutionary reconstitution of society at large or in the common ruin of the contending forces....."

I was enthralled. The power of the language, the clarity of Karl Marx's and Frederick Engels' vision gripped me. I thought about the world I myself was growing up in. The Manifesto seemed to describe the reality of my world perfectly. We were dirt poor farmers struggling with hundreds of other farmers, loggers, millworkers and other working people to keep our noses above water. Yet I could see all around me the wealth of the elite few. The Manifesto helped me understand where the wealth of the elite came from: The unpaid labor of tens of millions of working people.

The common denominator of all of us who were poor, or near poor, is that we struggled just to get back from the wealthy elite a larger share of the wealth we had created whether it was a 10 gallon can of pure grade A milk, a Douglas fir log, or an ingot of pure steel. The only way to end this dawn to dark exploitation was to unite, rise up and abolish the system of capitalism and institute a new order, socialism.

Six years later, I returned to Sequim at the end of my freshman year at college and plunged into the summer farm work, milking the cows twice daily, mowing, raking, and baling the alfalfa and hauling it into our barn.

The Communist Party club met monthly in the living of our old farm house up on Bell Hill. For several years, I had been sitting in on these meetings along with others in my generation. We also joined in the discussion.

Vivian Gaboury, leader of the club asked what the Club should take on as a summer project. Various ideas were tossed around. I spoke up. "The town of Amherst has a fair on the town common every year. The Quakers set up a peace booth. It created quite a stir."

"That's a great idea," Vivian exclaimed. "We could set up a peace booth at the Clallam County Fair in August. I'll check with the Fair administration on how we do it. We could set it up in the name of the 'Ad Hoc Committee To End Nuclear Testing.'"

Vivian secured space in one of the exhibition barns. I painted a mural based on the Prophet Isaiah, "And they shall pound their swords into plowshares and their spears into pruninghooks; nation shall not lift up sword against nation. Neither shall they study war any more."

We staffed that booth every day throughout the fair and many thousands of fairgoers stopped to pick up our literature and chat with us including a large contingent of my high school classmates, all of them young women, who were fascinated to see such a unique booth decorated with my art. All of them seemed very attractive to me. Proof that our Club was on the right side of history came a few years later when President John F. Kennedy joined with the Soviet Union in banning atmospheric nuclear testing.

After the fair, Vivian fixed me with her large, bright blue eyes and said, "Tim, we think it is time you joined the Party. What do you think?"

I nodded. "I agree. Yes, I would like to join."

It was as simple as that. I didn't agonize. I didn't need to think about it.

I am a member, still, and plan to be for as long as I live.

What attracted me to the Party and why have I remained a member?

• The Communist Party USA has a unique "united front" strategy to unite the majority of our people, to defeat the corporate ultra-right that seeks to destroy the labor movement, drive down workers wages and benefits, strip us of benefits like Social Security, Medicare and Medicaid to satisfy their profit greed.

• The Party has a proud history of fighting racism expressed in the slogan, "Black, Brown and White, Unite. Same Class, Same Fight." It stands against all forms of hatred and bigotry sown by the banks and corporations. These parasites suck super-profits from racist oppression. White supremacy is the capitalist class' most effective ideological weapon to split, divide, and weaken the working class. Anti-communism is another weapon of the monopolies and rightwing extremists for destroying working class unity.

• The CPUSA defends the Bill of Rights from ruthless attacks by the Republicans, who seek to take away our voting rights, and all other rights protected by the Constitution.

• It is a Party of grassroots action that joins in mass mobilization, that unites with other mass organizations including labor unions, civil rights and civil liberties organizations, the immigrant rights movement, the environmental movement, and grassroots forces of the Democratic Party.

• The CPUSA is a Party that embraces peaceful coexistence and opposes war, militarism, and all forms of aggression against other nations.

• It upholds the ultimate goal of socialism when the mass of the people will decide to "alter or abolish" the tyranny of monopoly capitalism and establish socialism. The working class---which is a majority of the people in our country---will then own the means of production and operate it in the interests of the people.

• It fights for these basic changes through peaceful means and does everything in its power to avoid

violence and provocation. Yet it also upholds the right
of oppressed and exploited people to defend themselves
when the wealthy elite unleashes its forces of coercion
upon us.

• Are we perfect? Far from it. The greatest error during
my tenure in the Party was our failure to join in the
struggle to end bigotry and hatred directed against Gays,
Lesbians, Transgender and Bisexual people. It was Gay
and Lesbian Party members who fought this error in the
Party and pushed through the correction. We seek to
educate ourselves, to raise our political consciousness
through reading, study and discussion. The class struggle is a constantly changing confrontation and requires
creativity and readiness to change our thinking in the
face of new realities. We call it a "science" and it is. But
it is also an art that rejects clichés and dogma.

• My membership in the CPUSA is more than the
embrace of Marxist theory or grassroots mass action.
It is a way of life. It is embracing working class culture.
It is loving folk music and folk dance that expresses
working class values. It is art and literature that celebrates labor and our multiracial, multinational working
class. It is a culture that reflects love of our brothers and
sisters, rejoicing in their victories, sorrow over their
defeats and a determination to rise once again until
victory is won.

• Above all, the attractive power of the Party lies in
the women and men of all races and nationalities who
belong to the Party. Anyone who observes the CPUSA
in action will see that it is a multiracial organization, a
rainbow. They are a most beautiful collective, modest,
sociable, smart in the application of mass strategy and
tactics, fearless in the face of intimidation, always seeking to raise our spirits and fighting unity. Some of them
I have profiled in my books.

I would be remiss if I did not invite you to join the
Party, or if you once belonged and then drifted away,
or quit for whatever reason, to come back. I have never

doubted that we are destined to win a sweeping victory in the future. Just how long that struggle will take depends on how united we are, how well we mobilize, how determined we are to turn people out to vote. We have no choice but to stand and fight for a massive defeat of the ultra-right whether we win that victory now or sometime in the years ahead. It is the key to defending democracy and everything else we hold dear.

About the Author

Tim Wheeler has been a news reporter since 1966 working for the *Worker, Daily World, People's Daily World*, and now the online *People's World*. He served as Washington Bureau Chief of the *Daily World* and its successors for twenty-five years and as Editor of the paper in New York City for eleven years. Most of those years he, and his wife, Joyce, and their three children, lived in Baltimore, Maryland. Joyce Wheeler, Tim's wife of 56 years, died of Alzheimer's disease, March 21, 2019. Tim Wheeler continues to live on the family farm in Sequim, Washington, where he grew up. He is politically active in all the progressive causes he can find time for. He still writes for the *People's World*.

CPSIA information can be obtained
at www.ICGtesting.com
Printed in the USA
BVHW080820020720
582412BV00002B/12